The Happy Writer:

Your Secret Weapon Against Rejection, Dejection, Writer's Block, And The Emotional Pitfalls Of The Writing Life

by

Writer's Relief, Inc.

Helping writers prepare and target their submissions since 1994

The Happy Writer: Your Secret Weapon Against Rejection, Dejection, Writer's Block, And The Emotional Pitfalls Of The Writing Life
Copyright: Writer's Relief, Inc.
Published: January 2014
ISBN: 978-0-9913015-2-2
Publisher: Writer's Relief, Inc.

ALL RIGHTS RESERVED. No part of this manual may be reproduced or transmitted for resale or use by any party other than the individual purchaser, who is the sole authorized user of this information. Purchaser is authorized to use any of the information in this publication for his or her own use ONLY. All other reproduction or transmission, in any form or by any means, electronic or mechanical, including photocopying, recording, or by any information storage or retrieval system, is prohibited without express written permission from Writer's Relief, Inc.

LEGAL NOTICES: While all attempts have been made to provide effective, verifiable information in this manual, neither the author nor publisher assumes any responsibility for errors, inaccuracies, or omissions. Any slights of people or organizations are unintentional. If advice concerning tax, legal, compliance, or related matters is needed, the services of a qualified professional should be sought. This manual is not a source of legal, regulatory compliance, or accounting information, and it should not be regarded as such. This publication is designed to provide accurate and authoritative information in regard to the subject matter covered. It is sold with the understanding that the publisher is not engaged in rendering legal, accounting, or other professional service. If legal advice or other expert assistance is required, the services of a competent professional should be sought. Due to the nature of publishing and varying rules regulating related activities in many fields, licensee and/or purchaser must accept full responsibility for determining the legality and/or ethical character of any and all business and publishing transactions and/or practices adopted and enacted in his or her particular field and geographic location, whether or not those transactions and/or practices are suggested, either directly or indirectly, in this manual. As with any business and publishing advice, the reader is strongly encouraged to seek professional counsel before taking action. NOTE: No guarantees of income or profits are intended or promised in this publication. Many variables affect individual results. Your results may vary. Writer's Relief, Inc. has no control over what you may do or not do with the information contained in this publication and therefore cannot accept responsibility for your results. You are the only one who can initiate the proper action in order to succeed in publishing your work.

Published by: Writer's Relief, Inc., Wood-Ridge, NJ 07075

© Writer's Relief, Inc., 2014

Table Of Contents

Introduction   1

Part One
Let's Get Started   7
Your Self-Assessment: Where's Your Head At?   9
Could You Be Self-Sabotaging Your Writing Career?   13
Considering Other Possibilities   17
  Is Your Chair Killing Your Creative Buzz?   18
  Are You Writing The Write Way?   20
  Looking At Diet: The Breakfast Of Writing Champions   23
  Sleep Your Way To The Top   26
  End Your Eyestrain   30
Changing Your Mind-Set: Working From The Inside Out   33
  Five Famous Literary "Failures"   34
  Famous Author Rejection Letters   38
Set Yourself Up For Success   43
  You Are What You Think   46
  Is Your Inner Critic Destructive Or Helpful?   49
  Make The Power Of Gratitude Work For You   51
  Think BIG By Starting Small   54
  A Little Patience Goes A Long Way   57
  Send Guilt A Big Fat Rejection Letter   60
  Build Confidence In Your Craft   63
  Our Very Best Tip For Changing Your Mind-Set   65

Part Two
Taking Charge Of Your Creativity   71
  Prepare Your Writer's Block Tool Kit   72
  What To Do When You Get Stuck   75
  Jump-Start Your Muse   78
  Look To Your Dreams For Inspiration   81
  Create A Prewriting Ritual   83
  When Copying Is Good For Your Career   86
  Step Out Of Your Comfort Zone   88

Part Three
Examine Your Beliefs About Rejection 93
   The Eight Rs Of Rejection 94
   What Does A Rejection Letter Mean? 98
   How Should Writers Deal With Rejection Letters? 102
   Famous Author Quotes About Rejection 104
   How You Can Turn Acceptances Into Rejections 106
   Turn Rejections Into Acceptances 108
   Mental Strategies For Coping With Rejection 112
Some Final Thoughts 115

Part Four
Resources On Our Website 121
Are You Ready To Develop Your Author Platform? 123
Our Invitation To You 125

Introduction: Who We Are And Why You Should Listen To Us

Writer's Relief is an author's submission service, and we've been helping creative writers make submissions since 1994. We're a highly specialized service with expert knowledge of the publishing industry.

We help book authors find agents.

We help poetry, short story, and essay writers get published in literary journals.

We also do a fair amount of congratulating, advising, strategizing, encouraging, consoling, and cheering on. The writing life is full of ups and downs. Tears and triumph. Our submission strategists are our clients' support team for when times get tough—and they *always* get tough at one point or another. Even for the best writers.

What we share with you in this book are the general strategies that get results for our clients. These are solid pieces of practical advice that have been put to the test over and over again. In other words, the numbers show that the strategies we offer are proven to work. We hope you'll give them some consideration, even if you ultimately decide to embrace different strategies.

You may notice a certain amount of "quiet repetition" throughout this book. We want to assure you that this is intentional. Some of the ideas we put forward are reiterated throughout this book in multiple ways. We've done this because changing phrasing or looking at the same idea from a new angle can lead readers to reach their own insights at different times. What works for one writer may not work for another. Also, we want the ideas of positive thinking, healthy living, and optimism to stick in readers' minds. We've found that occasional repetition of core ideas can help facilitate that goal.

We've been working with writers for many years, and we've been part of our clients' lives through all their emotional ups and downs. Our clients are regularly published in lit mags. They get many, many manuscript requests from literary agents based on strong query letters. And some go on to earn offers of representation. But no matter their successes, they all face the doldrums, the disappointments, and the difficulties of being a writer.

Many of our clients report that they struggle less often with rejection and despair because they have joined Writer's Relief. When we manage the submission process for a writer, rejection becomes less personal. And when rejection is less personal, our clients generally find they have more enthusiasm, energy, and drive. We believe this partnership frees our clients to become better writers. Many clients see their acceptance rate increase as their confidence increases.

If you're interested in knowing how Writer's Relief can help you (we can manage as much or as little of the submission process as you like), just find us online or give us a call. We're easy to reach. But of course you do not *need* a Writer's Relief submission strategist managing your submissions for you in order to succeed. If you've got the energy, dedication, focus, and time for making submissions, you'll be just fine. For now, just enjoy this book. We hope it will help you stay motivated, encouraged, and inspired.

Please get in touch with us and let us know what you think! We would love to hear your story of overcoming the emotional hurdles of the writing life. We might even use it on our blog!

Happy reading!

Ronnie L. Smith, President
Ronnie L. Smith, President
Writer's Relief, Inc.
(866) 405-3003
www.WritersRelief.com

WRITER'S RELIEF EST.
AUTHOR'S SUBMISSION SERVICE 1994

Part One

Changing Your Mind-Set

How To Stay Positive, Inspired, And Encouraged

Let's Get Started

We don't need to outline for you all of the reasons that the writing life can be emotionally difficult. But here are just a few of the obstacles you may be facing from within:

- Isolation and loneliness
- Hopelessness
- Intense criticism
- Jealousy
- Rejection letters
- You name it

The problems of the writing life are not going to go away—not even if you're a *New York Times* best seller. But while you can't change the nature of the writing life, you CAN change how you feel about it.

In this book, we're going to give you the tools you need to feel better about tackling the difficulties of being a writer.

But first let's get one thing out of the way about the nature of disappointment and despair: It doesn't last forever.

Let's start by taking an honest look at your state of mind right now. Before you can move forward, it can help to know where you are.

Your Self-Assessment: Where's Your Head At?

Career burnout can affect people in any profession, but writers face special challenges. Writers often start out with high ideals and unrealistic expectations, picturing themselves churning out works of art and happily reaping the rewards.

But the reality of the writing life often doesn't gel with these high hopes. It takes time, hard work, and self-discipline to become successful—usually *lots* of time and *lots* of hard work—which can eventually lead to career burnout.

How To Know If You're Suffering From Writing Burnout

Burnout is different from procrastination or writer's block. We all have days when we just want to be a couch potato. But if you're consistently avoiding your work, feeling disillusioned, or suffering from vague aches and pains, you may be feeling burned out—a problem that can strike anyone, whether you're a writer, a doctor, or a lint inspector. Before you toss your laptop out the window, consider the following:

It's important to recognize the early warning signs of burnout. You may avoid writing altogether, either by flat-out refusing to pick up a pen or procrastinating.

Some writers blame their wayward muse or stare blankly at the computer screen before giving up. Others are able to write but are dissatisfied with the results...consistently. Signs of burnout can also include a lack of energy, a sense of disillusionment, depression, irritability, and a generally negative outlook.

Burnout can affect writers physically as well. It may manifest itself in headaches and backaches, joint pain, eating and sleep disorders, and physical exhaustion. All in all, burnout is not a pleasant state of mind—and it's not a pleasant physical condition either.

What Causes Writers To Burn Out?

It's easy to get overwhelmed if you maintain a superhuman pace for too long. The brain and body can only take so much. And if your work takes up too much time, you may not have time for family, friends, or hobbies.

By not recharging your mental (and physical) batteries, you're pretty much guaranteed to hit the wall at some point. Writers are also susceptible to certain negative aspects of the writing life: rejection letters, a lack of control (the waiting game; being dependent on editors or agents), financial issues, a lack of social support, and/or solitude.

The first step to coping with burnout is recognition. Once you've identified the problem, you can take steps to alleviate the symptoms.

Six Tips For Writers Dealing With Career Burnout

1. Don't define yourself by your successes or failures. Even if your short stories haven't been picked up by lit magazines or you've just received your fiftieth rejection letter from an agent...you are still a writer. No one, and nothing that happens, can change that about you.

However...you are also a person with other interests and talents and aspects to consider, so give yourself a break, explore other passions, and see yourself as a whole person—

not someone who is solely defined by rejection or publication credits.

2. Focus on the positive. It's hard not to be negative when you're feeling disillusioned and depressed, and negativity is an easy place in which to dwell and stagnate. Remember why you started writing in the first place, and make a list of all the positive aspects of the writing life.

3. Adjust your expectations and goals. Most writers juggle full-time jobs and have to make time to write on the side. Add the demands of family, friends, and all the other obligations of life, and it's easy to feel overwhelmed. Review your writing goals and make sure they're realistic (you've got to sleep sometime!). Once you've got a schedule you can live with, stick to it and reward yourself for any progress you make.

4. Find a better balance between writing and free time. Designate time to be with your family and friends, exercise, meditate, or simply indulge in a marathon of your favorite TV show. Mindless chores like vacuuming or washing dishes can clear your brain too—and you might feel better when things are tidy. By scheduling "you time," even if it's only in small increments, you might feel recharged enough to get back to the hard stuff.

5. Concentrate on your health. Make a good night's sleep a priority whenever possible, and eat a little better. Get your eyes checked if you're suffering from headaches or eyestrain, or take a brisk walk if your back is aching. More tips on staying healthy follow.

6. Rediscover your passion. Read work by your favorite authors or poets, those who inspired you to become a writer in the first place. Or take a trip to the library and browse the aisles simply for the pleasure of seeing all those books in print. One of them could be yours someday!

The Long Run: Longevity In Your Writing Career

Unfortunately, writing is often a career dependent on deadlines, and it's not always easy to take time out for mental and physical health. Overdoing it is an unavoidable part of many jobs, including writing, but it isn't conducive to good, consistent, creative output. And the inevitable result is career burnout.

Before that happens, take control of your life and your career by scheduling downtime, setting realistic goals, focusing on the positive, taking care of yourself, and asking for help when you need it.

Could You Be Self-Sabotaging Your Writing Career?

Many professional writers credit their success to both hard work and being in the right place at the right time. But sometimes being in the right place and working hard simply aren't enough. Unless you're truly open to success, you'll have the deck stacked against you even before the cards are dealt! Here are five signs that you might be self-sabotaging your own writing career.

Sign #1. Writing doesn't make you happy anymore. Maybe, at some point, you truly loved your work. But lately your stories feel flat. You find yourself twitching and getting distracted when you're supposed to be working, and when you finish a piece, you don't get that lovely glowing feeling that follows a big accomplishment.

SOLUTION: Get back to basics. Stop and assess where your listlessness is coming from. What used to make you happy about writing that isn't making you happy now? Make a list of what you love about writing, and read it before you sit down to work. Then, focus on what you love, and let the rest go.

Sign #2. You don't feel your writing is strong. Perhaps you have many publication credits, perhaps you have none. Either way, you're feeling down about your writing—and that feeling is leaking into the actual words you write.

SOLUTION: Time to reevaluate how you look at your work. Take drastic measures to do whatever it takes to begin to love your own stories and poems. Ask friends and family to tell you what they like about your work. Make a list of what you like about it. When you love your writing and are confident in your own talent, your chance at success improves!

Sign #3. You sit down to write, but there's no inspiration to be found. You want to write but your fingers remain quiet on the keyboard. How will you become a well-regarded writer if you're not writing? You're caught in a downward spiral.

SOLUTION: Time to reinvigorate your muse—but there's absolutely no reason to do it alone. Find a local poetry reading series—even if you don't write poetry, you'll be inspired. Join a writing group or a book club. Being around words that inspire you—or even words that fail you and make you long for something better—will revive your muse. Also, consider going to an art museum or a concert, or take a glassblowing class. Sometimes changing the direction of your creativity, if only for a moment, will reinvigorate your passion for words.

Sign #4. A great opportunity comes your way—maybe a literary agent is interested in a book project, or an editor wants to publish one of your poems, but she or he requests a few revisions. You worry. You worry so much that you end up sending multiple emails to the agent or editor in a single day. You call and pester. When you finally do get in touch with the agent or editor, you're cranky and suspicious—you question everything. You feel you're not getting enough attention. You think you're being mistreated. You wonder why literary agents and editors aren't taking you seriously and why good opportunities dry up.

SOLUTION: Your nerves may be blocking your path to success. Time to relax—but also to be aware of your own proclivity to botch situations that could help your career. When in doubt, treat people as you want to be treated—with trust, patience, and kindness.

Sign #5. You've finished your book, short story, poem, or essay, and after a period of procrastination, you send your work to a handful of literary agents or editors. Rejection letters ensue. You think: Well, I'll send it out to a few more people, but then you don't actually do it—or you do very little. Your work, which you suspect is quite good despite your handful of rejections, languishes and remains unpublished.

SOLUTION: Rather than relying on vague goals (I will send out my work), it's time to make concrete, specific goals and stick to them (I will send my book to X number of agents per week/month). Tell others who will hold you accountable to check in with you and encourage you to stay on track (and remember to be nice to them even when it feels like they're nagging you). Then, even if the prospects look glum, you won't lose momentum.

BOTTOM LINE: These five signs of sabotage are symptoms of deeper issues. If you're self-sabotaging your writing career, it's time to do some deep introspection. Although you're going after success, is there something that's keeping you from getting it? Write in a journal, listen to your own inner voice, and learn what may be blocking you.

Considering Other Possibilities: The Hidden Problems That Can Contribute To A Glum Mood

Before you begin digging up all your childhood memories to discover why you may have lost some of your creative drive, there are a few other things to rule out.

Sometimes the trigger for a bad mood isn't mental. It could be physical. We cannot be emphatic enough about this: Without a healthy body, it's extremely hard to stay energetic, motivated, positive, and focused. So don't underestimate the importance of staying healthy in order to have a good, successful writing career.

As a writer, you need to give yourself every possible advantage for success. You don't have to be a professional bodybuilder or supermodel; we're simply suggesting that making an effort to be your healthiest self—that is, as healthy as you as an individual can be—might be helpful in improving your mood, outlook, and productivity.

Let's look at some common, hidden problems (and simple fixes) that could be affecting your writing life.

Writer's Relief

Is Your Chair Killing Your Creative Buzz?

These days, many of us lead a sedentary lifestyle—especially writers who make their living seated for untold hours at computers. Aspiring, nonprofessional writers have it even worse—before spending long hours writing at home, they've already spent a full day at another job. All this sitting is bad for your body, your brain health, and—as science now suggests—your creativity.

The link between the body and the creative mind is becoming better understood. In *The Creative Habit*, Twyla Tharp explains: "The chemistry of the body is inseparable from the chemistry of the brain. Movement can stimulate anyone. I can't say enough about the connection between body and mind; when you stimulate your body, your brain comes alive in ways you can't simulate in a sedentary position. The brain is an organ, tied integrally to all the other systems in the body, and it's affected by blood flow, neural transmission, all the processes you undergo when you put your body through its paces. You're making it work differently, and new directions can result."

So how can novelists, poets, and short prose writers increase their activity level—thereby increasing creativity and the quality of their work—short of joining a gym and adopting a dreaded exercise regimen?

There are a myriad of virtually painless ways! Here are a few:

Do seated exercises. Okay, so you're really averse to anything remotely resembling "real exercise." How about a few simple body movements you can perform without leaving that beloved chair? Lift your legs, stretch your arms, rotate your ankles. Every little bit of movement helps.

Stand at your computer. There are a growing number of people who espouse the benefits of a stand-up desk. While standing, you naturally tend to move a lot more, and it's also good for posture, circulation, and reducing fatigue. You can easily test the concept by placing your laptop at eye level on a box on your desk.

Get up and stretch every hour. Make it a point to get up and stretch every hour or so. As long as you're up, walk down the hall and then walk up and down that staircase you'd rather avoid. Not only do these little trips invigorate and refresh...they burn calories to boot!

Dance to the music. You don't have to be Twyla Tharp to reap the benefits of dancing. When you're working at home, put on some music every so often and just move to it. Rock to Aerosmith. Sway to Mozart. March in place to John Philip Sousa. Moving to music not only spurs the creative juices, it makes you happy!

Take a hike! According to a study referenced in *Scientific American*, participants who spent four days hiking without electronic devices scored nearly 50% higher on creativity tests than a control group. Fifty percent is a *huge* difference. It may not be possible to go hiking in the woods for four days, but it is possible to incorporate the concept into your daily life. Take a few moments each day to stroll around your yard or the grounds of your apartment complex WITHOUT your cell or smartphone. The walking will fulfill the need for more movement, while the daily observing of the world around you will serve to inspire your writing.

Writer's Relief

Are You Writing The Write Way? Healthy Computing For Writers

Writers don't risk too many job injuries, but long hours at the computer can take their toll. Many writers wonder how they can avoid eyestrain, carpal tunnel syndrome, headaches, fatigue, back pain, and muscle cramps.

Welcome to the wonderful world of writing! Spending long hours in front of the computer may translate into productive writing sessions (which can lead to positive feedback from literary agents and editors), but it may also lead to physical discomfort. The following tips may help you work more comfortably while you're plugging away at your book, story, poem, or essay.

Adjust your environment. It's easier to work in a well-ventilated room with plenty of fresh air. Consider adding a few plants to filter the air and brighten your workspace. Adjust the room temperature so that it's neither too hot (think: sleepy) nor too cold (think: stiff fingers). It's also a good idea to wipe down your keyboard, mouse, and phone with antibacterial wipes once in a while (or more frequently, depending on how many little hands touch your computer equipment).

Adjust your equipment. Keep your computer monitor placed just below eye level. Positioning it too high or too low can cause strain on your neck muscles. The screen should be approximately an arm's length away from you. If you have trouble seeing the characters on the screen, try adjusting the brightness and/or contrast first.

Invest in an ergonomically correct chair, one that provides lower back support and can be adjusted to your height requirements. If your feet do not rest flat on the floor, use a footrest to relieve stress on your leg muscles. Check your local office product store for the latest and greatest.

Protect your eyes. Take frequent eye breaks to reduce eyestrain (more on this in a moment). Physically walk away from your computer, or look away from the screen and focus on an object farther away. Close your eyes occasionally and keep them closed for several seconds. Or try slow eye rolls, following the shape of an imaginary clock.

Use proper lighting to reduce glare on your monitor. This may take some experimentation on your part as you adjust blinds, overhead lights, and/or desk lamps. You can also purchase anti-glare computer filters.

Protect your wrists. Pounding on the keyboard can cause discomfort, as can gripping the mouse too tightly. Use a light touch on both. While typing, keep your arms level with the keyboard and use them, rather than your wrists, to move your hands across the keyboard. Some people find that a wristrest (or a rolled-up towel) helps keep their forearms level, while others use them only as an actual rest between typing. Persistent pain and/or numbness of the hands or wrists could signal a more serious problem, such as carpal tunnel syndrome, so check with your doctor.

Protect your neck. If you spend a good amount of time on the telephone, try using a speakerphone or a hands-free headset. Cradling the phone between your neck and shoulder is a surefire way to strain your neck muscles.

Take frequent breaks. Even maintaining perfect posture and using all the latest gadgets can't protect you from achy muscles if you don't give your body a break once in a while. Roll your neck and shoulders periodically, and get up at frequent intervals to stretch. Better yet, jog around your desk and then send off a few queries. When you return you'll be refreshed and ready to work again.

Looking At Diet: The Breakfast Of Writing Champions

We all know certain foods contribute positively to your physical health, and some foods contribute positively (in inches) to your waistline. But did you know that some foods can support brain function—and maybe even make you a better, happier writer?

Antioxidants, like those found in fruits and vegetables, offer disease- and age-fighting power to keep your creative impulses firing at top speed. Blueberries are said to be especially powerful.

Omega-3 fatty acids (from fish oil and flax) are said to boost your brain's gray matter. That's like building muscle in your mind. Prepare to do some heavy mental lifting...or just impress people with your mental calisthenics.

Choline is a nutrient found in egg yolk or milk that can help ward off senility. Choline also keeps your memory going strong, so you can actually remember whether your character was wearing a red shirt or a blue one twenty pages ago!

Folic acid. One study found that adults taking regular folic acid supplements demonstrated better cognitive function, especially in memory and critical thinking. So if you're really having trouble getting past a problematic plot point, it may be time to supplement!

Chocolate lovers rejoice! According to WebMD: "A study by food scientists found that the antioxidant concentration in a cup of hot cocoa was higher than that found in either red wine or green tea." Of course, getting your antioxidants from veggies may be a better bet. But next time your spouse gives you "that look" for drinking hot chocolate, you can say, "I'm doing it for my brain!"

Green tea is good for your brain too. People who drink green tea regularly fare better mentally when it comes to aging. This is happy news for writers—especially if you're the type who stays up into the wee hours working on a manuscript; your green tea can multitask by keeping you both awake AND young! Plus, moderate amounts of caffeine are said to boost concentration as long as you don't overdo it.

Sugar. No, we're not talking about the powdery white dusting on doughnuts or the stuff that your grandpa dumps in his coffee until it's thick as sludge. Nor are we talking about fake sugar substitutes. Your brain may not love what we call "sugar," but it does love glucose. Glucose is what your body makes out of sugar and carbs. And a little lift in glucose can boost your concentration and alertness. Just be sure that when you reach for sweet, you're reaching for healthy sweet: blueberries, oranges, etc. Your brain will get its glucose fix and some antioxidants too!

Breakfast. We know you don't want to admit it, but your mom was right. Breakfast counts. Eat a moderate breakfast with protein and whole grains, and you—like countless human guinea pigs—may find that your concentration gets a boost. Just don't eat too much or you'll get sluggish.

Supplements. There's a lot of back-and-forth these days about supplements. But research suggests that vitamins B, C, E, magnesium, and beta-carotene may be helpful.

The Disclaimer

Do we even need to say this? We're creative writers, not nutritionists. So you should hear yourself saying, "What's up, Doc?" before you alter your diet to power your brain.

Still, common sense doesn't require a medical degree. So eat right, sleep deeply, and drink plenty of water.

And if you don't know what it means to eat right, take your cues from Michael Pollan (author of *In Defense of Food*), who takes all the food advice out there and breaks it down into three simple rules:

1. Eat REAL food (as opposed to "food-like substances").
2. Not too much.
3. Mostly plants.

A healthy body usually brings about a healthy brain. And that makes for powerful writing and a more buoyant mood.

Sleep Your Way To The Top: Your Mood And Your Sleeping Brain

Writers of ages past produced their masterworks without a computer, or even a typewriter. Chaucer, Cervantes, Shakespeare—each made manifest his creative genius with only a quill in hand. Likewise, they managed to write without electricity, without indoor plumbing, without access to cars or telephones or the Internet.

What they did need to support their intellect and creativity was food, water, human relationships…and sleep. Without enough sleep, good health, good living, and good writing are impossible.

Why Your Sleeping Habits Matter And Improve Your Writing

Science confirms that sleep can make you smarter and more creative. In a study referenced in *National Geographic Daily News*, people who took naps that plunged them into REM sleep performed better on creativity-oriented word problems. Scores of other scientific studies document the importance of sleep to good health—both physical and mental.

For the amateur or professional writer, too little sleep has numerous negative effects. When tired, you have less "get up and go."

Does this scenario sound familiar? Let's say you have to start writing, but you just can't get off the couch: "I'll sit here another half hour, and then I'll tackle the work."

Finally, you force yourself to sit at your desk. You stare at the computer screen—but ideas, words, and phrases do not blossom. Your brain is just not working. You put your chin on your open palm and stare blankly out the window. Without enough sleep, you do not think clearly.

After great struggle, you finally manage to get a few paragraphs written. You turn off the computer and think, "I'll take a look at this later." When later arrives, you read what you'd written and discover the grammar is poor, punctuation is missing, and you've used a word or two unartfully. Without enough sleep, you make lots of mistakes.

If this sounds like your writing life, the problem may have more to do with your sleeping habits than a lack of motivation.

How To Sleep Better (And Write Better)

Don't fight your body clock. Some people just aren't cut out for going to bed at 10 p.m. and waking up at 6 a.m. Having a shorter night's sleep supplemented by a late-afternoon nap works well for many. Others need a solid eight hours of shut-eye. Base your sleep schedule on what your body wants rather than on the clock.

Exercise. The importance of regular exercise for good sleep is well-established. For sleep purposes, though, it is important that you don't exercise late in the day. Exercise speeds up your metabolism; that's great for getting you through the day with full energy, but as you enter the hours before going to bed, you'll want your body slowing down, not speeding up.

Unwind. For the thirty or so minutes before bedtime, turn off the TV, the computer, and yes, your portable devices. You want to be emptying your mind of controversy and stress-inducing thoughts. Take a long, warm shower. Meditate for a few minutes. Have a cup of chamomile tea. Limit this time to quiet conversation or listening to soothing music—anything that tends to calm rather than stimulate.

Make your sleep space inviting. Analyze your bed and bedding—sheets, blankets, pillows—and choose each element for maximum comfort. Paint the bedroom a calming hue, not a stimulating "hot" color. Make your bed and bedroom so tranquil and inviting that you can't wait to go to bed!

Diminish noise. The most common cause of sleep disruption is noise. Many people swear by having white noise in the background. There are small devices that not only mask street noise but generate their own soothing sounds such as falling rain, gently crashing waves, and babbling brooks. A simple fan can achieve the same result, albeit with a monotonous hum.

Reconsider sharing your bed. Consider not giving your pet access to your bedroom during sleep time. Pets can disturb sleep time without your necessarily knowing it. What pet owner hasn't been roused out of a sound sleep by a cat jumping up on the bed in the middle of the night or by a dog circling and circling until it settles down?

Manage the light. As delightful as a sunny morning can be, it is not so grand when sunlight pours through your window three hours earlier than you wanted to wake up. Your bedroom should be as dark as possible during sleep hours. Position your bed so that sunlight won't land on the pillows. If you have blinds, pull the strings so that the slats are pitched upward rather than downward. If your curtains are lightweight, consider getting a thicker, light-blocking type, or install roller shades to be pulled down when you go to bed.

Sleep is every bit as important to a writer's success as the desire to tell a story and the mastery of language. In a writer's arsenal, every letter of the alphabet is important. But as it turns out, no letter is more important to creative writing than the Z-z-z-z-z-z-z!

End Your Eyestrain

You probably know what it's like to suffer from eyestrain. Writers are often the victims of computer-related maladies such as headaches, blurry vision, itchy or dry eyes, and eyestrain, but there are steps you can take to ease suffering and protect your eyes from further stress.

How To Avoid Eyestrain

1. First, get a proper eye exam, update your glasses or contact lenses, and rule out any physical problems. (Studies indicate that those who spend a good deal of time in front of the computer are more at risk for glaucoma.)

2. Evaluate your workspace. Make sure your computer screen is at a comfortable viewing angle; working too close to the monitor can cause eyestrain and headaches (not to mention neck and back pain).

3. Adjust your background and font size. It's nearly impossible to read white text on a black background, and straining to read a 10-point font is asking for trouble. If you write in the evening hours, check out an application called f.lux, which makes the color of your computer's display adapt to the time of day—warm at night and more like sunlight during the day.

4. Reduce glare. Use indirect or reflective lighting when possible, and invest in an anti-glare filter for your computer monitor. Make sure your screen is at a 90-degree angle from any direct light source.

5. Take frequent breaks. Take a short walk, head to the break room for a cup of tea, or try this simple exercise if you can't leave your desk: Shift your focus from your screen to an

object that is at least twenty feet away, and focus on it for several seconds before returning your eyes to the screen. Repeat on a regular basis throughout the day.

6. We've already talked about eating right for your mental acuity and your mood. But your food choices can affect your eye health as well. Eating right, staying well-hydrated, and exercising regularly will have a positive effect on your eye health, and so will getting a good night's sleep.

7. Try these two techniques to both relax and exercise your eyes (from Dr. Marc Grossman, OD, LaC, Eastern Region Director of the Optometric Extension Program Foundation):

> Palming Exercise
>
> Rub your hands together until they feel warm (about fifteen to twenty seconds). Then place your cupped hands over your closed eyes, being careful not to touch your eyes with the palms of your hands. The fingers of each hand should overlap and rest gently on the center of your forehead. Don't create any unnecessary pressure on your face. If your arms get tired, rest your elbows on a table. Sit quietly for one to two minutes with your hands over your eyes. The more relaxed you become, the blacker the darkness you will see with your eyes closed.
>
> Near-Far Focus
>
> Hold your thumb six inches from your nose and focus on it. Take one deep breath and exhale slowly. Then focus on an object about ten feet away. Take another deep breath and slowly exhale. Repeat this process fifteen times.

Writers are especially prone to eyestrain and know that it can lead to loss of productivity and even long-term health problems. When writing is more comfortable, you'll be more inclined to stay enthusiastic about it—and your drive to work will improve.

If you are certain that the reason your spirits are flagging has nothing to do with your chair, your diet, or your sleep patterns, then it's time to start looking inward.

In our next section we will give you fantastic tips that will help you improve your mood—and your writing.

Changing Your Mind-Set: Working From The Inside Out

You're a writer: You know your most powerful tool is your brain.

But it can also be your worst enemy.

We're about to share with you some fantastic techniques for taking charge of your mood and your future.

But before we do, let's look at some stories about writers who seemed to have been failures, only to discover that they were on their way. Changing your mental state will be hard work, but we hope the promise evidenced in these stories will keep you motivated to be on *your* way.

Writer's Relief

Five Famous Literary "Failures" And Why They're Awesome

All writers can produce clunkers. Novelists have done it, short story writers have done it, poets have done it, and even car-naming "authors" have done it. Yes, Chevrolet's old Nova didn't sell well in Spanish-speaking countries with a name that translates to "doesn't go"!

But sometimes, a book that is regarded as a clunker when it first comes out goes on to be revered and appreciated. Here are just a few books that were subjected to some terrible reviews when they came out. "Clunker" is in the eye of the beholder!

Wuthering Heights **by Emily Brontë:** *Wuthering Heights*, that angst-filled classic, was not unanimously loved. Charlotte Brontë wrote an introduction to a later edition of the book that makes no bones about needing to defend the novel against its critics. Reviewers claimed the characters were vulgar and incredible. The story was deemed wild, out of control. These days? Emily's book is regarded as a breathtaking, moody work that is loved for the very reasons early critics hated it.

Moby Dick **by Herman Melville:** Melville's whale of a tale was a flop in his time. Though its characters speared whales for lamp oil, many of the author's peers much preferred to read by the light of its burning pages. The book was on the market for forty years and sold only a few thousand copies. These days? Even if you haven't tackled the tome, you know that "Call me Ishmael" is a household phrase.

Leaves of Grass **by Walt Whitman:** Our boy Walt really hit on something with his long ramble of free verse that celebrates the human spirit… And as far as some of his first critics were concerned, the thing he hit on was a perfect lack of good taste. Whitman's poetry was revolutionary when his book hit the shelves, and it was also misunderstood. These days? *Leaves of Grass* is required reading that marks a moment of shifting cultural and poetic values.

Lolita by Vladimir Nabokov: *Lolita* has always been a controversial novel, and for good reason! It was initially passed over by American publishers before the author decided to seek publication in France. The book got off to a stormy start. Badly presented (the book was allegedly full of typos and didn't have much of its publisher's support), *Lolita* was reviled and even banned. But when it hit the shelves in America, it only took a few days before the book was into its third printing. These days? *Lolita* will always be a difficult book, but it's been named to many "best books ever" lists.

Emily Dickinson's poetry: This beloved American poet published fewer than two dozen poems during her lifetime, so she doesn't get a book title on our list. Her first collection wasn't published until after her death. During her lifetime, her poetic ideas were not only questioned but belittled. Some early readers of her poetry adored it, but many found her poems to be off-putting and not-poem-like (because it isn't a poem if it doesn't rhyme, right?). It wasn't until the twentieth century that readers and critics began to appreciate her as a modern poet.

All this reminds us of a joke that gets passed around in writing groups:

Q: How many critics does it take to change a light bulb?

A: Critics can't change a light bulb. But they'll watch you do it and tell you a hundred things you could have done better.

So next time you're sitting in your critique group listening to people bash your book, remember that even the most well-known authors were sometimes panned!

But What About Books That Really *Are* Clunkers?

Sometimes even great writers pen crummy books. It happens. It should happen. The difference between a bad writer and a good writer is that a good writer knows what to throw out before the public reads it.

Clunkers are a natural part of the writing life. Some experiments don't succeed, and that's nothing to be ashamed of! Writers should take risks, should go out on a limb, should break new ground—even at the expense of being ridiculed.

But if critics can't tell whether or not your clunker is a masterpiece, how can you?

How To Spot A Clunker Or A Literary Lemon

Trust your instincts. You often know in your heart of hearts when you haven't done your best work.

Spend time apart. It can be hard to see a clunker if you're not emotionally distant from the work. So it's good practice to get away from a project for a while and then come back to it with new eyes.

Get feedback. Listen to honest critiques from friends, your writing group, and, most importantly, from professionals. Remember that the level of critique you receive is usually on par with the level of the writer giving it. Being critiqued by a person who has published a handful of stories is different from being critiqued by a successful veteran who writes in your genre. Your family, friends, and fellow critique-session attendees might mean well but also might be a bit too gentle.

What To Do With Your Clunker

- Save the best parts for possible use in future projects.

- Sit down and make a list—thorough and honest—of the project's weaknesses. Seeing weak points on paper means you can't ignore them or let your subconscious mind "forget" them. Better work will result!

- If you do publish a clunker, accept the results with grace—whether the response is good or bad.

The Importance Of Clunking

Don't let fear of writing a clunker hold you back or hinder your creativity. In some circles, writers refer to what's called "MFA-type writing." This is writing that's solid, articulate, and interesting…but also safe, a little dull, and, at its deepest levels, lacking in some essential passion or drive. It's said that this type of writing is born from students who are trying to win over their workshop peers and avoid criticism.

In other words, taking risks is key to success. An occasional clunker can be good for the writer's soul—and the world!

Writer's Relief

More Stories Of Apparent Failure: Famous Author Rejection Letters

Even well-known writers faced their share of rejection before they made it big.

Many new or mid-level writers have received nasty or rude rejection letters. But when famous author rejection letters come to light, people laugh and say, "What were those editors (or literary agents) thinking?" Many big names faced the same kind of adversity (and even hostility) in rejection letters that you may be facing now. Famous author rejection letters teach us a lot!

When you get a harsh rejection letter, keep these famous author rejections in mind.

Check out these reported excerpts from *real* famous author rejections:

Sylvia Plath: There certainly isn't enough genuine talent for us to take notice.

Rudyard Kipling: I'm sorry, Mr. Kipling, but you just don't know how to use the English language.

J. G. Ballard: The author of this book is beyond psychiatric help.

Emily Dickinson: [Your poems] are quite as remarkable for defects as for beauties and are generally devoid of true poetical qualities.

Ernest Hemingway (regarding *The Torrents of Spring*): It would be extremely rotten taste, to say nothing of being horribly cruel, should we want to publish it.

Obviously, these famous author rejection letter phrases have gone down in history for how outrageous they seem to us now. The comments probably had more to do with the mood of the person writing them than with the quality of the work.

It seems odd to us now that Plath, Kipling, Ballard, Dickinson, and Hemingway were rejected so cruelly. But these comments show us that famous author rejection letters are no different than not-so-famous author rejection letters!

Thank goodness these authors kept writing and submitting. Ask yourself: Where would we be if they had given up? We would have missed a lot of important literature!

Famous Author Rejections: Hitting A Dry Spell

Feel glum over oodles of rejection letters? Check out these stats of famous authors' failed submissions. (Please note that the examples below are often referenced and we've done quite a lot of research, but as with so many things, there's always a chance for error. Do not cite this article for your academic thesis! Go to the original sources.)

- John Grisham's first novel was rejected 25 times.
- Jack Canfield and Mark Victor Hansen (*Chicken Soup for the Soul*) received 134 rejections.
- Beatrix Potter had so much trouble publishing *The Tale of Peter Rabbit*, she initially had to self-publish it.
- Robert Pirsig (*Zen and the Art of Motorcycle Maintenance*) received 121 rejections before the book was published and went on to become a best seller.
- Gertrude Stein spent 22 years submitting before getting a single poem accepted.
- Judy Blume, beloved by children everywhere, received rejections for two straight years.

- Madeline L'Engle received 26 rejections before getting *A Wrinkle in Time* published—which went on to win the Newbery Medal and become one of the best-selling children's books of all time.
- Frank Herbert's *Dune* was rejected 20 times before being published and becoming a cult classic.
- Stephen King received dozens of rejections for *Carrie* before it was published (and made into a movie!).
- James Lee Burke's novel *The Lost Get-Back Boogie* was rejected 111 times over a period of nine years and, upon its publication by Louisiana State University Press in 1986, was nominated for a Pulitzer Prize.

The Most Rejected Novelist In History?

Author Dick Wimmer passed away on May 18, 2011, at 74 years old. He received 160+ rejections over 25 years! He spent a quarter of a century being told "no."

He could have quit after 20 years, or 150 rejections, and no one would have blamed him. But he kept at it (maybe he had his own list of famous author rejection letters to keep him going!).

Finally, his novel *Irish Wine* (Mercury House, 1989) was published to positive reviews. *The New York Times* called it a "taut, finely written, exhaustingly exuberant first novel."

Assuming the author's submissions were well-targeted, how could 160+ people have passed over Wimmer's book? And what does that mean for YOUR writing career?

Wimmer's self-proclaimed legacy is of being the "most rejected novelist," but we think his legacy is hope and persistence.

The Moral Of The Story

Before you decide that being rejected now means you're going to be rejected forever, remember that it's important to keep focused on the future. Rejection doesn't have to be a roadblock; it only stops you if you let it turn into despair and melancholy. Instead, regard nuisances as a bump in the road and you will find a way over them with poise and optimism.

Set Yourself Up For Success

Now that you understand, on a practical level, that disappointment now doesn't mean disappointment forever, it's time to start taking steps that will help you to feel better about your chosen occupation.

As writers, we've been told time and time again that we need to develop thick skins, deal with criticism constructively, persevere in the face of a thousand rejection slips. And we've all heard the stories of how many well-known authors were turned down by countless editors, only to later publish a best seller.

But the reality for most of us is this: Success is hard to measure in the world of writing, and it's up to you to create a realistic measure for yourself. Take a minute to examine your ultimate goals and determine how to stay focused and positive during the difficult process of submitting your writing.

Do you feel you'll be a failure if you don't produce the next great American novel or if you publish only seven poems instead of the fifty you promised yourself? If your happiness is tied to reaching certain goals, maybe it's time for some reevaluation. Sure, Sylvia Plath's genius was inextricably tied to her despair and depression, but for the most part, a dejected, deflated writer will produce dejected, deflated writing. It's time to take charge of your happiness so you can take charge of your writing.

Explore your inner voice. This is the voice inside your head, orchestrating your thoughts and progress. If it says, "You're not good enough," how can it not affect your writing? Be kind to yourself. If you're new to writing, change "not good enough" to "learning the ropes." If you've been at it for years and are still hitting a wall, take a good hard look at the critiques and suggestions you've received. Take a class, try a new genre, explore writing groups that offer solid advice and constructive criticism. Above all, put aside your ego long enough to really hear what experts say about your writing.

What would make you happy? An angry, pessimistic, irritable writer may hang all his or her hopes for happiness on publication. But chances are that if this writer gets published, he or she will simply become an angry, pessimistic, and irritable author with a publication credit. It's kind of like winning the lottery—you may suddenly have a million dollars, but the problems in your life are still there: You're still afraid of spiders, still estranged from your grown children, still suffering from heartburn, and the cat still throws up on the carpet nearly every day. The process of writing should be a joy in itself. Publication is the icing on the cake.

Are you being realistic? Get-rich schemes don't work, and magical shortcuts to publication don't exist. Writing takes time to develop, like a good wine develops depth and character with age. This doesn't mean that you have to be in a nursing home to finally reach your goals, but looking for instant gratification won't help either. Patience, persistence, constant and well-targeted submissions—these are what will move you toward your publishing goals.

Set yourself up with small, reachable steps, and celebrate the completion of each one. *I will work on my synopsis for thirty minutes. I will get a good night's sleep so I can work on a poem early in the morning while everyone sleeps. I will let the machine take my calls for the next two hours, and I will eat a healthy lunch for energy. I will identify the problem* *with my antagonist and fix it.* Each step leads to the next, and the path will slowly unfold before you.

You Are What You Think

Émile Coué de la Châtaigneraie was a French psychologist who is famous for his mantra-like affirmation: "Every day, in every way, I'm getting better and better." He believed that repeating this at the beginning and end of each day could influence a person's unconscious thoughts and lead to greater success.

Creative writers can also use this technique. (Don't worry, positive affirmations aren't just for the New Age or hippie set. Any writer can take advantage of this practice without having to wear Birkenstocks or light incense!)

In a field where rejections are a common occurrence, a little positive self-talk can be a valuable tool to stave off self-doubt and fear of failure.

An affirmation is a positive phrase (written in the first person, in the present tense) that states a goal or a truth that you want to impress upon your mind. For example, if you wish to live in the present, consciously, and not dwell on the past or the future, you might use "Be here now."

The theory is that by clearing your mind and repeating this phrase to yourself out loud, you can create this belief in your conscious mind. A writer might use an affirmation like "I am creative and talented" or "I will keep submitting my work until I am published."

Some writers use brief quotes from authors who inspire them, while others use highly specific mantras: "Clichés have no part in my writing."

At the very least, what writer couldn't use a little pep talk once a day?

How Writers Can Use Affirmations

1. Keep them brief and limited. Focus on one or two phrases until you feel you've incorporated them into your psyche. Then you can move on to others.

2. Use the present tense. Instead of "By next year, I will be more famous than Toni Morrison," focus on today. "I have a special gift with words." Or "I am evolving as a writer every day."

3. Don't lie. Your subconscious will not be receptive to flat-out lies. If you aren't already on the *New York Times* list, don't use an affirmation like "I am a best-selling author." Try "I am moving toward my goal of writing a great novel."

4. Practice your affirmations routinely. It can be the first thing you do when you wake up and the last thing before you go to sleep. Some people prefer to say them while looking in the mirror; some require solitude and a peaceful frame of mind; and others find that repeating their affirmations during everyday routines (like a commute or a morning walk) helps the practice become automatic.

5. If you do yoga or meditate, this is an ideal time to incorporate positive thoughts and goals, while your mind is focused.

6. Write down your affirmations. You can post them on your computer, stick them on the bathroom mirror, or carry them with you. The act of writing them down and seeing them in print will help solidify them in your mind.

7. This isn't a mantra so much as a tip for positive living. Choose positive words when you're thinking through your everyday tasks. Read more about word choice here:

Here are some examples of positive affirmations specifically for writers:

1. I am a writer. Writing is my art.

2. My writing is strengthened by constructive criticism from others and from myself.

3. Rejection is a valuable part of the process.

4. I am creative. My words flow easily and beautifully.

5. I write every day, with confidence and enthusiasm.

6. I can visualize success, and I have the patience and talent to reach it.

7. I can be a successful writer and a successful (mother/attorney/cab driver).

8. I can create vivid images and put them down on paper.

9. I am responsible for my own destiny.

10. I am not at the mercy of my muse; I can find inspiration at any time.

When you believe that whatever happens is for your own development and success, nothing can bring you down, and you don't have to have lived in an ashram to use positive affirmations.

Creating a positive mind-set will not only help you achieve your goals as a writer—it's a powerful strategy for all areas of your life! Why not use all the tools at your disposal? Your writing will thank you.

The Happy Writer

Is Your Inner Critic Destructive Or Helpful?

Writers know that constructive criticism is an essential part of becoming a better writer. We've come to terms with the role rejection plays in the submission process. And we bravely pass around our latest efforts at our monthly writers group, knowing that we're opening ourselves up to a possible unfavorable comment or two...at best. We're proud of ourselves for accepting this external literary critique as an unavoidable part of the publishing industry.

But how do you deal with the negative comments and thoughts that come from within? How to silence that internal scallywag who likes to whisper in our ear and sabotage our confidence? "Who in the world are you trying to fool with this 'I'm a writer' act? You've got to be kidding!"

Don't let your inner critic derail your writing career. First, determine whether this internal voice is stemming from truth or from fear.

A general "Your writing is terrible" may stem from fear—the fear of failure, rejection, embarrassment. Perhaps, deep down, you fear you've made a bad career choice. Or you're worried that you've been fooling yourself about your talent. It's only natural to hear this negative voice in your head from time to time, telling you that you're risking your family's financial security or that no one will ever respect your work. This voice creates self-doubt, which doesn't help much when you're trying to be productive.

There are other insidious voices that do a writer no good. One is Ms. Procrastination, who likes to suggest, in silky tones, that you'll have plenty of time tomorrow to work on a new story. Her cousin, Ms. Compassion, softly whispers, "You must be so tired. Why don't you take a little nap and try this writing thing again tomorrow?" And then there's Mr. Guilt. "Don't you think your house/kids/dogs/garden could use a little of your attention right now? And you selfishly want to write?" You can ignore these voices or argue with them, replacing their negative messages with words of encouragement, but you mustn't let them distract you from your goals.

On the other hand, if the voice is saying, "Your character is not believable," maybe it's time to take a good look at the character in question. After all, your inner critic actually represents your own instincts as a writer, and we all need to pay attention to what we instinctively recognize as good writing versus bad. It's best if you can squash the voice of reason until you've been allowed to muddle through a first draft—never let the inner critic stop the creative flow—and when it's time for revision, you can then pay attention to your instincts and see what words of wisdom emerge.

You'll always have an internal dialogue in your head—we all do—but it's important to learn which messages to take seriously and which messages are self-defeating. Listen carefully and determine what's true, what's destructive, and what's just plain silly. Befriend that critic, learn from it, and keep writing.

Make The Power Of Gratitude Work For You

When life hands you lemons, do you make lemonade or a scrunchy, sour face? As a writer, do you let the long hours, the isolation, and the rejection letters get you down? Or do you embrace every part of being a writer with the power of gratitude?

There are many benefits to focusing on the positive side of the writing life, and they're not just mental perks. Your attitude can make you a better writer AND improve your career track.

1. Say thank you. As a professional writer, you have worked hard to build publication credits. You've poured your heart and soul into your writing, and you're no shirker when it comes to accepting constructive criticism and making revisions.

Your author website is up-to-date and professional, and you carefully market yourself through social media and other venues. You've endured months of waiting for editors and literary agents to respond to your queries, and you don't let rejection get you down.

But have you said thank you?

If you have had the joy of having a poem, short story, or essay appear in a literary journal or magazine, take the time to send a note of thanks to the editor who published your piece. If you've published a novel, why not thank the cover designer who made your book "pop" or the copy editor who carefully went over every single word of your 350-page novel?

Writer's Relief

Despite our mothers' admonitions, most people simply forget the power of expressing thanks to those who help us in our writing journey. But by doing so, people will remember you.

Not only will they remember you as a person, but you will stand out as a professional and considerate author. You'd be surprised how many people forget this simple courtesy and how much it's appreciated. And, who knows, that editor you so thoughtfully remembered may remember YOU the next time you submit a piece.

Even if you haven't reached the point of having editors or cover designers to thank, there are other people who contribute to your writing journey: a special teacher or librarian, maybe a particularly insightful member of your critique group who went above and beyond, or a parent who encouraged you every step of the way, no matter what.

It costs nothing to say thanks. And it feels great!

2. Be grateful for rejection. A rejection letter is proof that you have put yourself out there as a writer. You have taken that oh-so-difficult step of submitting your work, and you are working toward getting it published.

Rejection letters mean that you believe in your work strongly enough to offer it up for consideration, and you are passionate about your writing. Go you!

Rejection letters offer a great opportunity for writers to learn what editors or agents are looking for, what you should work on, and the direction you might want to take.

If a busy agent took the time to send you a note, then your work merited the courtesy of a reply, however brief. Embrace these gifts of rejection and learn from them. Challenge yourself to do better, and congratulate yourself for walking the walk, not just talking the talk!

3. Be grateful for gratitude—a powerful tool that focuses your attention on what matters most. Most people will agree that a positive and grateful attitude enhances our quality of life in general, and writers can benefit from this attitude as well.

You may be feeling the weight of deadlines, rejection, or writer's block, but if you step back and evaluate why you are a writer, you'll find the answers are all positive: Because I can't NOT write. Because I am creative. Because I have things to share. Because I have a unique voice. Because writing makes me feel fulfilled.

The next time you get bogged down by the negatives, take a moment to write down all the wonderful things about being a writer. What it gives you. How it helps you. The positive outcomes you envision. Allow yourself to be grateful for your gifts.

You will likely be motivated and inspired after reviewing the reasons behind your desire to be a writer, which can also get your muse revved up and ready to go.

So there you have it. How lucky you are to have a passion and a creative expression! At Writer's Relief, we are also grateful—grateful for our clients and grateful for those who visit our blog. And after the assault of Superstorm Sandy, we are even more thankful for all the good things in our lives we would otherwise take for granted—like electricity and a roof over our heads!

Stick To Promises You CAN Keep—Think BIG By Starting Small

Stay motivated and encouraged by making this important promise to yourself (repeat after us): "This year I promise to always THINK BIG."

It's a great time to be a writer. The world is going through incredible changes right before our eyes, and whether the changes are good or bad, the truth is that turmoil and upheaval birth creative genius, innovative ideas, and new directions.

Visualize yourself actively creating this year, rather than passively sitting back to see what happens in the publishing industry. Everyone will have a different idea of what BIG is—whether it's overcoming a fear of rejection and sending out that very first submission or landing a big-time literary agent—but it's important to make thinking on a grand scale a part of your everyday life.

When it comes to the writing life, the easy thing to do is stack negatives: It's hard to make a living as a writer; the odds of publication are daunting; my sister hated my short story; my wrists hurt.

A successful writer will have vision that transcends the negatives. I'm doing what I truly love to do. I have talent. Writing is my creative outlet. I see myself doing BIG things in the writing arena. And by thinking this way, it's so much easier to actually achieve big goals.

Some writers will make a checklist of small, attainable steps as building blocks to their ultimate goal. Others will just sit down and get to the business of writing a novel (or a play or a poem) until it's complete. The key is COMMITMENT to these goals. See yourself as a flourishing and dedicated writer and then make it happen, any way you know how.

Don't let yourself be intimidated by big dreams. Remember that old joke about how to eat an elephant: "One bite at a time." Approach your writing goals the same way, and don't let that big bad elephant send you running from the room.

Maintain your enthusiasm. If you remind yourself each day to think BIG, this kind of positive attitude can actually become a part of your nature; eventually, you will naturally see yourself as a successful writer.

You won't be derailed by rejection letters, writer's block, or editors who won't publish your short story. Instead, you'll see this as a necessary part of the process of writing. Rejection and roadblocks won't define you as a writer; they will inspire you to forge ahead.

Reward yourself generously for your dedication. For some, crossing an item off a list can be tremendously rewarding. For others, a pint of ice cream or a trip to the botanical gardens is reward enough for finishing a difficult chapter or sending out a new batch of query letters.

Use positive reinforcement on yourself—it works well for children and pets, so why not writers? Treat yourself kindly and with patience.

Don't set yourself up for failure. "If I don't write a novel and see it published by next year, I quit!" Instead, see yourself reaching attainable goals. "I'm going to get a rough draft of a novel completed by this time next year!" Don't make failure a possibility.

Always come from a place of excellence. Do your best work, always, and continue to expand and improve your skills. Take writing classes, read the classics, welcome constructive criticism. Know that even if you simply wrote one paragraph, it was an excellent paragraph—your best effort.

Embrace your career with joy and enthusiasm. You're a writer! Even if you spend eight hours a day at a mattress factory, that's just your day job. You're a writer! Your work inspires, motivates, challenges, and creates emotional reactions for your readers. What an incredible gift you have to share!

The bottom line. Whether you've got a four-page to-do list for the new year or one big ambition, frame your goals in a positive light and get started. If you get bogged down by plot problems or blindsided by a particularly scathing rejection letter, take a moment to bring your vision to the forefront. Visualize the BIG prize and see yourself taking it for your own.

A Little Patience Goes A Long Way: So Cut Yourself A Break

What is the secret to a long, successful career in publishing—full of many book publications, collections of poems and short stories, awards, and accolades for your creative writing?

While a select few folks get lucky—scoring major book deals with little or no writing technique or background—others must toil for years before finding success.

We writers take classes, go to workshops, shell out money for writing conferences, sit alone at our computers for hours, and make countless sacrifices, all in the name of achieving The Dream. We wonder: How much longer can we keep going? How much more can we give before we burn out? When—if ever—will we get a payout?

At the end of the day, one virtue may be the most responsible for the long-term success of life as a creative writer: patience. **The publishing industry is notoriously slow.** Gradually, the industry seems to be speeding up as technology improves. But right now there's no overnight, surefire way to build a career as a writer at a traditional publishing house. Some writers will self-publish or go to online-only publications to speed up the process a bit, but in the world of big, national publishing markets, slow and steady wins the race.

Here are a few reasons that patience is a top virtue of creative writers. If publishing with a major traditional publisher or even a small press is your goal, you'll need patience:

When you're crafting your creative writing. First, you'll need patience to learn the techniques of good writing. And you'll need patience when it's time to decide whether or not your work is "done." Many professional writers will shelve a project for weeks, months, or years before seeking publication, so that when they return to the project down the line, they'll be able to see it with new eyes.

When you're putting your submissions together. Patience is necessary to get through all the tedious hours of researching the best agents and editors for your writing and for preparing submissions. Lack of patience leads to shoddy submissions—and that, as everyone knows, leads to rejection letters.

When you're waiting for responses. Almost anyone who's serious about submissions has a story to tell about receiving a rejection letter years after a given work was sent. Literary agents and literary journal editors can get hundreds of submissions each week, and it takes time to read through all those letters and pieces.

When you're waiting to be published. Small literary magazines and journals—as well as big publishing houses—often have a schedule for publishing poetry, stories, essays, and books. Once you've signed your contract, your project will be in "take a number" mode. Some publishers stipulate that they have up to two years to publish a project from the date a contract is signed.

If you're submitting a book, by now you've waited years to write your manuscript, months (or years) to get an agent, and now you're supposed to wait again while your publishing house deliberates. Then, if your book is selected for publication, it can take months to draw up and agree upon a contract, then weeks for the accounting department to write your check (which goes to your agent, who must process it before you see it). It's a long, slow slogging toward publication (and payment). Better sit tight.

Patient writers are successful writers. Patience isn't necessarily passive—that is, it's not just about sitting on your butt and waiting for something good to happen. Patience can be a very active, demanding task—one that many writers must master.

Remember, you don't need to hit the *New York Times* list tomorrow (and you probably won't). Enjoy the journey of being a writer. You've earned the right to enjoy it by all your hard work and perseverance. With the right amount of patience, focus, and talent, success is within your grasp.

Writer's Relief

Send Guilt A Big Fat Rejection Letter

You know about writer's block. But did you know there's such a thing as writer's guilt?

The writing life comes with its share of guilt. Guilty feelings can come from needing to block off lots of alone time, from not making a huge income, and from many other sources. But there are healthy, constructive ways to work through the guilty conscience that can come with being a writer.

Check Out Our Four Solutions To Overcoming Guilt In The Writing Life!

1. You feel guilty turning down invitations because you need the time for writing.

PROBLEM: Aunt Petunia is hosting a barbecue this weekend to celebrate her daughter's graduation from preschool. Unfortunately, you had slotted that day to enter a short story in a contest you know you can win. You really need to stay in this weekend to write—but what if no one understands why entering this contest trumps little Betsy's grad party?

SOLUTION: If you were a lawyer and had to prepare for your upcoming motion, you wouldn't feel guilty. And you know that if the barbecue had been scheduled for the weekend of the World Series, baseball-obsessed Uncle Milton would have no problem RSVPing with a big, fat "no."

Admit to yourself that you work hard at your writing and you're passionate about it (and you shouldn't have to apologize for it!). So while you may not feel comfortable going into detail as to why you can't come see Betsy modeling her miniature graduation cap, let yourself off the hook and get some butt-in-chair time.

2. You feel guilty that you don't have a list of publication credits to justify the time and effort spent writing and submitting.

PROBLEM: You spend a lot of time working on your craft, but it still hasn't paid off in the form of significant publication. You're having trouble explaining to friends and family—or even yourself—why you're working so hard on your writing.

SOLUTION: Every published author started out as an unpublished author. While publication credits certainly help catch the attention of agents and editors, quality writing can be its own advocate. Keep writing, working on your craft, and submitting. Your next publication credit may be an asset to your cover/query letter—or the springboard to your writing career.

3. You feel guilty because you won't let everyone read your work (in one form of revision or another).

PROBLEM: You're faced with loved ones peering over your shoulder as you write or begging for a reading when you're really not ready. When they point out that you share your work with a writing group and/or submit to journal editors or literary agents, you're not sure how to explain why that's different.

SOLUTION: You have the right to ask for understanding. Explain that the opinions of friends and family can mean the most, so while you can deal with criticism from people in the biz, it could hurt deeply if your friends and family don't love your writing.

If the person seems genuinely pained by the lack of sharing, you can try a compromise: Consider allowing the person to read the work once you've deemed it ready to submit to agents and editors. Or let him/her read it "first" once the work has been accepted, before the book or journal edition is published and read by the masses. The important thing is that you, first and foremost, should feel good about the compromise. If not, your loved ones may just have to buy the book or publication to read your writing.

4. You feel guilty writing about inspiration gleaned from real life because of the other people involved.

PROBLEM: Cousin Ron splitting his pants at your sister's wedding was comedy gold, and you're eager to add it to the short story you're working on. And the pain of your loved one's passing is something you just need to write a poem about. But you want to avoid hurting anyone by revealing what might be sensitive information.

SOLUTION: Of course your creativity comes from real life, but that doesn't mean you have to needlessly embarrass or betray anyone. Take steps to disguise people…take a lot of steps. You can still write that scene about a man splitting his pants at a wedding—or was it a chaperone at a school dance? You get the idea.

If you do write a scene with direct connections to real life, remember that you can't unpublish your work. So if your catalyst for writing is anger or spite, you're probably better off writing that piece in your private journal (not everything needs to be published).

Build Confidence In Your Craft

It takes a certain amount of confidence to be a creative writer. The simple act of putting pen to paper can make a writer feel vulnerable, and at Writer's Relief, we know all about the courage required to submit your precious work to editors and literary agents. Anxiety and self-doubt can completely derail some writers; others will be more likely to procrastinate when it comes to writing and submitting. And for others, a lack of confidence can be a roadblock to creativity.

A confident writer is a successful writer—a writer who sees criticism as feedback and a rejection letter as a necessary part of the submission process. So how can writers build confidence in their craft and become more successful?

How To Be A More Confident Writer

Remind yourself why you are a writer. We're willing to bet you didn't become a writer for the money or the glamorous lifestyle... So it must be because you have a passion, a talent, a need to write, no matter what other people think.

Review your best work as evidence. Whether it's a towering stack of great short stories or simply one particularly perfect scene from a novel in the works, gather the writing you're most proud of and remind yourself of your talent.

Rejoice in rejection. Rejection letters from literary agents and editors are evidence that you are submitting your work, plugging away at your dreams. A writer without a rejection letter is a writer who hasn't had the courage to reach out.

Don't compare yourself to others. Your writing style, publication credits, background, inspiration—these are all uniquely yours. If you constantly compare yourself to "more successful" writers, you are doing yourself a disservice.

Step out of your comfort zone. If poetry is your strength, push yourself in a new direction just for fun—explore the world of short stories or personal essays and see if you have an undiscovered talent.

Let go of expectations. Try sitting down and just letting your writing come. Don't obsess over a perfect first sentence, and don't try to force a certain style if it doesn't feel natural. Just do what you love to do without putting pressure on yourself. Edit later, if you must.

Share your work. Whether you join a writers group or start submitting your work for publication, face the anxiety of what other people may think and deal with it. Even if you receive nothing but constructive criticism, you'll have faced a writer's biggest fear: putting your writing out there.

Tap into your fears and insecurities. A well-fed, complacent cat is more likely to sun itself than go hunting; writers can use the energy of their anxiety to get them off the couch and out there, hunting for a new idea or a new market. Fear and anxiety are energy—energy writers can use to their advantage.

Remember that as writers, we are works in progress. The more we write—the more we read, take classes, and study our craft—the better writers we become. As our skills improve, so does our confidence. So if you're serious about boosting your confidence as a writer, the best advice may be simply to *write*.

The Happy Writer

And Our Very Best Tip For Changing Your Mind-Set To Gain More Success

The writing life is tough: It can be hard to stay motivated when you're slogging along, alone, with nothing but the company of your rejection letters and the world's tiniest violinist playing sad music outside your window (okay, maybe not that last part).

If your goal is to be a career writer (that is, a writer who makes a career out of words), here's one trick that many successful writers found useful, even when they were just starting out, even when there was nothing to indicate that they had a future as a writer.

Let us put it simply:

Write Like It's Your Job...Even If It's Technically Not

Here's why:

If you want to be a professional, you have to start by thinking of yourself as a professional. This seems like a simple notion but it's not. How are we writers supposed to think of ourselves as consummate professionals when we work in our pajamas at odd hours, when an hour's hard work is staring into space and daydreaming, and when it's so easy to put aside our writing goals for the sake of family and friends?

The key to becoming a professional writer is believing that you are a professional writer—now, while the neighbors are outside having a pool party, while the kids are jumping on the bed, while nothing in your career looks quite like you want it to—yet.

No matter where you are in your career, you're always in a position to reset your mind-set to treat your own goals with the professionalism and respect they deserve.

When you demonstrate that you take your work seriously, others will take it seriously too. Even family members or friends who have doubted will—eventually—have to come around because your dedication, professionalism, and seriousness will convince them.

When you treat your work with professional courtesy and dedication, your mind-set will have a ripple effect. Having the support of nears and dears can be critical to success. You are the one who sets the tone for your career. Plus, when you treat your writing time as sacred and important, agents and editors are more likely to feel that (and see it in your words).

Here are some tips for treating your writing like it's your job:

Act like you're working for someone else. You know how being late for work can be a huge stressor—because who wants to get on the boss's bad side? But then, when it's time to sit down to write (or get up early in the morning to squeeze in some writing time), it's easy to say, "What difference will fifteen minutes make?"

If you pretend you're working for someone else—someone whom you're professionally obligated to do right by—then you might muster a little more diligence.

If creating an imaginary writing boss doesn't work for you, consider treating yourself as your boss. When it comes to writing, is there anyone you should be trying to impress who is more important than you are? We think not.

The Happy Writer

Don't call it an office; call it a studio, playroom, or imaginarium. Some successful people will often say things like, "I've never worked a day in my life." Now, most of us know that's poppycock, in a way—Edison says genius is more perspiration than inspiration. But the mind-set of approaching the work is what we're getting at. Work hard and do so because you enjoy it. Attitude will help you go far.

Pay yourself for writing. Very few (realistic and practical) people decide that the best way to make a fortune is to write a novel. There's a reason writers end up with a reputation for being short of funds.

Even if you're low on dough, you can create a system to pay yourself for your work. Maybe you write by the hour (and pay yourself one Hershey's kiss per hour). Or maybe you are paid by the word (with an extra minute in the shower for every five hundred words you write).

Whatever you decide, when you treat your writing like it's a job—even if it's not actually paying money yet—there's a better chance that real paychecks will be coming down the line.

Caveat: This particular technique might not work for everyone. Some people don't want their writing to feel like work, ever. Some people don't distinguish between work and play when it comes to creative pursuits.

Okay—so let's say after reading all of this, you're thinking, "My mood isn't my problem. I'm just not feeling inspired."

Continue reading to learn great techniques for recharging your creativity.

Part Two

When You Get Stuck

Jump-Starting Your Creative And Professional Drive

Taking Charge Of Your Creativity

Our muses are fickle. But with practice, we can learn to manage them. This next section will give you some great advice for energizing, corralling, and protecting your muse.

Let's start by looking at what you can do even before your muse begins to gaze off into the distance with a blank look of boredom.

Writer's Relief

Prepare Your Writer's Block Tool Kit

Writer's block: two little words that make any writer shiver. If you're used to feeling helpless when writer's block interrupts you, we have a solution: Prepare for the worst before you're blocked.

Pack the following supplies in your emergency kit, and next time you're feeling blah and uninspired, you'll be prepared to go into battle with the block.

Map of your escape route: A toxic environment can attack your muse. Fight off the doldrums with some new scenery. Prepare a list of inspiring places that you can get to quickly the next time writer's block hits. A change of pace might revive your desire to do the hard work of writing.

Do you enjoy nature? Bring your notebook to a local park or even your own backyard. Do you love people-watching? Plug in your laptop at a local café, or keep a bus schedule handy and grab the next roundtrip ride. Make your emergency escape plan, and when writer's block strikes, don't stew and fester in the doldrums. Just go!

Pain killer: Like a throbbing pain, writer's block can worsen with stress. You need an antidote to get you through until you're feeling better again. Give yourself some temporary relief by walking away and doing something that relaxes you or makes you happy. To prepare, make a list of things that relax you or clear your mind: taking a bubble bath, doing a jigsaw puzzle, jogging, etc. Rather than working to get inspired, use this list next time you need to get some breathing room and return to the drawing board.

Flashlight: When you're caught in the dark, everything can seem gloomy. You could be standing in a roomful of people

The Happy Writer

who are having the same trouble you're having, but you feel alone. Darkness of the spirit can skew perspective and make you feel like all's lost. Be ready for darkness in your writing life; it's unavoidable even for the best writers.

Make a list of your achievements—everything from "I finished my manuscript" to "I was nominated for the Pushcart Prize." Refer back to it when you're feeling glum. Also, read books by other writers; many authors have penned encouraging books that talk about overcoming setbacks. Buy a few to keep on your bookshelf, and read a few pages to shine some light on your situation. Find some quotes that inspire you, and keep them close to your desk—just like you keep a flashlight nearby in case the lights go out. Then, when darkness falls, you'll be ready!

Flare: At some point, all writers need help (with editing, marketing, brainstorming, and moral support). When truly in need, send out a flare for others to see, and help will be on its way. Prepare for the future by nurturing a support system today. Join and be actively involved in an online or local writing community. Meet people and help them when you can. Then, when *you* need help, you can be sure it will be there for you, ready and waiting.

Plan a list (even if it's a short list) of people you feel comfortable talking to about your writing. Maybe it's your best friend, a sibling, or a partner from your writing group. If there's a particular character, plot, or issue you're stuck on, ask someone for ideas. Even if you don't solve the problem, there will most likely be something in the conversation that will help you brainstorm later.

Sustenance: Similar to the food and water you would store in an emergency kit, your brain needs nourishment to defeat severe cases of writer's block. Go through your music library and make a few playlists of inspiring songs. They could be songs that you find energizing, relaxing, or that bring out particular emotional responses. Also, use sticky notes to flag inspirational passages in books and literary journals that you admire. The next time you're feeling really desperate, you won't have to think about how you'll lift your mood. Instead, you can just do it!

The Happy Writer

What To Do When You Get Stuck

Most writers have a secret stash of half-finished short stories, manuscripts, or poems—discarded when the author came to a screeching halt somewhere in the middle of things. If you've ever gotten stuck in the middle of a story or can't find the last line of a poem, here are a few steps to help you get moving again.

Step 1: Step back. Take some time away from your project and let your subconscious work on the problem in its own way. You may walk away for a month or thirty minutes, but the break will often bring clarity.

Step 2: Use physical energy to stimulate mental energy. Run around the block, vacuum the house, walk the dog, or chase the neighbor's kids—then come back to your project refreshed and oxygenated.

Step 3: Examine underlying problems. Perhaps you've hit a roadblock in the middle because deeper issues exist overall. Or maybe that last line of your poem isn't forthcoming because the poem itself needs a new direction. Sometimes we become emotionally attached to a character, scene, or plotline that doesn't actually work well with the piece as a whole.

"When I find myself frozen—whether I'm working on a brief passage in a novel or brainstorming about an entire book—it's usually because I'm trying to shoehorn an idea into the passage or story where it has no place."
—Jeffery Deaver

Step 4: Revisit the areas of your work that flow smoothly. Going over the good parts can help unblock the problem in other areas.

Step 5: Don't try too hard. Cut yourself some slack, stop trying to be perfect, and just start writing. Sometimes genius happens when we least expect it.

"Don't get it right, just get it written."
—James Thurber

Step 6: Hand it over. An objective writer friend, professor, or critique group member whose opinion you respect can sometimes spot the problem right away.

Step 7: Read other people's work. Find inspiration in the classics or a modern poet you admire.

"Read a lot. Write a lot. Have fun."
—Daniel Pinkwater

Step 8: If all else fails, take out a classified ad: LOST: One Fickle Muse!

Some Other Tips

For short stories and novels, write a synopsis to help clarify the plot and theme. You can also create a more detailed outline to sort things out and help you see what you need to do to move the story forward.

If your problem is that you have too many ideas, grab a notebook and jot down everything—later you can sort through and decide what to use, what to scrap, and what might tie everything together.

You can also try writing prompts to get things moving again. If your book or short story falls flat in the middle, ask yourself, "What would happen if my main character did _____ instead of _____?" Or "What is my character's motivation for _____?"

Jump-Start Your Muse!

We've all felt it. The blank look that creeps across our faces as we stare at the computer screen. The utter lack of inspiration for writers. The lack of fire. Sometimes we can't bring forth even a scrap of creative genius, and sometimes a once-inspiring idea suddenly goes stale. It's something that happens to every writer, and everyone has his/her own way of dealing with the problem. We've put together a few ideas we hope will help get the word-party started.

How To Come Up With Ideas For New Or Existing Projects

Change of scenery. Yes, we know. You hear this all the time, but if it works, it's worth a try. Jump on a bike, hop a train, pull on the sneakers, and go someplace different. It may be a new coffeehouse down the street, an unexplored neighborhood, even a tropical vacation, but the change of scenery may be just what you need to get a fresh perspective.

Eavesdrop. Blatantly and unabashedly eavesdrop on interesting conversations. Take notes. If nothing develops (and you don't get caught), at least you will have honed your dialogue skills.

Carry a notebook. Sometimes our best ideas strike out of the blue, so be prepared and carry a notebook to capture them. Take notes on things you observe, capture interesting characters you encounter on the subway, or record great one-liners you overhear. Sometimes even one word can evoke an entire scene as you review your notes later.

Read. It can be an author whose style you admire or *Gerbils Monthly* magazine. Read something that inspires you, or check out something you've never considered reading before.

The Happy Writer

If you've always been too embarrassed to buy a cheesy tabloid, do so now with the confidence of a good excuse: We'll call it research. See what ideas are generated by the outrageous headlines, and get out of your own head for a while.

Take a class. Most writers spend an ungodly amount of time in front of a computer screen. Try taking a class that has nothing to do with writing, such as tai chi or cooking. You may meet some interesting people and develop new ideas from the setting. And you'll be more relaxed as you create the perfect soufflé.

Free write. Sometimes the act of writing itself can get things started. Get a blank piece of paper and just start filling it up with whatever comes to mind. Be silly, shocking, or close your eyes and try to connect with the other side. Whatever it takes.

Give yourself a deadline. Generate a false sense of panic and tell yourself you have two hours to (fill in the blank). Sometimes working under pressure creates the best product, even if you know you won't be fired if you miss the deadline.

Take a break. If you've worried an idea half to death, take a break and work on something else. If the idea is worth salvaging, it will eventually come back to life. If it doesn't work after several breaks, it might be time to start over with something new.

A new angle. Research your idea from an entirely new perspective. Writing a short story about a farmer's disastrous harvest season? Try approaching it from a new angle, such as a farmer's daughter's joyful wedding in the middle of a disastrous harvest season. Want to write about dogs? Imagine your subject from different perspectives, such as dogs from a vet's point of view versus a child's point of view. Brainstorm all possible angles surrounding your idea, and see what develops. If you're unable to revive your passion for the once-hot idea, it may be time to scrap it, either temporarily or permanently. Our world provides a rich feast of ideas for the creative mind, and when the right concept comes along, you'll know it. And write it.

The Happy Writer

Look To Your Dreams For Inspiration

Awake or asleep, creative writers are dreamers. But what's the connection between writing and the dreams that come of their own accord at night? And how can a writer tap into this rich source of inspiration and creative energy?

If a writer can forge a link between the imagery and symbolism of their dreams and the power of their own writing, creative sparks will fly. Sometimes a snippet of a dream is all it takes to inspire a poem, story, or novel.

Examples Of Stories That Were Sprung From Dreams

Richard Bach was moved to write the first few chapters of *Jonathan Livingston Seagull* after he heard "a disembodied voice" whisper the title in his ear. But it wasn't until eight years later, after a dream that featured the famous seagull, that he was able to finish his hugely popular novella.

Stephen King, too, has looked to dreams for inspiration. In *Writers Dreaming* by Naomi Epel, King says, "...when I got road-blocked in my novel *It*, I had a dream about leeches inside discarded refrigerators. I immediately woke up and thought, 'That is where this is supposed to go.'"

Mary Shelley wasn't even fully asleep—she lay down and closed her eyes and was haunted by a ghastly mental image that inspired her to write *Frankenstein*. "I began that day with the words, 'It was on a dreary night of November,' making only a transcript of the grim terrors of my waking dream."

The creative energy of a writer's dreams can generate forward movement. Maurice Sendak, in *Writers Dreaming*, says, "What dreams do is raise the emotional level of what

I'm doing at the moment. They add color or counterpoint to the work, acting as an almost symphonic accompaniment to what I'm doing."

How To Make The Most Of Your Dreams

1. Pay attention to your dreams and jot down notes about them as soon as you wake up. You may be able to glean general ideas—themes, plot, characters, or settings—from the wild tangle of images, if not the full concept of a novel. Dreams can certainly be a jumping-off point for the creative process.

2. Try making a conscious effort, before going to sleep, to be present and aware in your dreams that night. Some people describe being aware of dreaming while in the midst of a dream and are able to participate more fully in the dream or even direct it to a certain extent—something that would certainly take some practice, but what fun it would be!

3. If you're suffering from writer's block or faced with a seemingly insurmountable plot problem, concentrate on the problem right before drifting off. Your subconscious may work to resolve the dilemma overnight and either reveal a resolution in a dream or upon awakening.

Simply be aware of the process—and the power—of dreaming to tap into that creative energy—and use it to your writing advantage!

Create A Prewriting Ritual

Think Of It As A Warm-Up

When you're prepping for a career as a writer, you're in training the same way that a professional athlete is in training. You put in long hours. You practice. You perfect. You practice again.

Sure, there have been athletes who wowed the world without seeming to do much actual prep (Babe Ruth has a reputation for doing half the preparation that professional baseballers put in today). But most of the time, to get to the pro level, you've got to take your warm-ups seriously.

Warming up your body before a big workout is like warming up your brain before a few hours at the computer. Getting into the right frame of mind helps. If you want to make the most of your writing time, consider a warm-up ritual.

Establish A Marker Between Your Daily Life And Your Writing Time

Some writers like to create a clear line between their time spent doing everyday tasks and their time spent writing about the things that matter deeply to them. You can do this by:

- Lighting a candle
- Retreating into the "sacred" space where you write
- Saying a prayer
- Meditating
- Writing down your worries on an index card and symbolically locking it away
- Reading a meaningful or inspiring book that's sacred to you

- Setting an intention (to make the most of your time, to stay focused, to write generously, etc.)

Whatever you choose, enter into your writing time with a sense of the sacredness or solemnity of—or joy for—the task before you. When you're writing for something "bigger" than you, you may find that your writing gets "bigger" too. And when you've made a dedicated effort to focus and not let the distractions of life get in the way, you may find your creativity improves.

Activities That Move Your Brain Into A Creative State

Once you've set your intention and created a defining line between the worries of your non-writing life and your creative intentions, you might consider spending just a few minutes doing a creative activity that warms up your generative muscles before you dive into the heavy work of writing.

Here are a few things that some writers do to prepare their brains for a major creative output:

- Read a poem or passage by a writer you admire
- Sketch
- Listen to music
- Make a list of anything (colors, incidents, emotions, synonyms for a given word, etc.)
- Free-write in a journal
- Get your blood moving with jumping jacks

Sometimes creating a prewriting ritual can help alleviate writer's block. Your brain will begin to anticipate a successful writing session even before you set your fingers to the keyboard or your pen to the paper.

While taking extra time to warm up before you write might seem difficult, the results can be very rewarding; they'll show up on your pages and in your readers' reactions to your work.

Plus, by loosening up your creative muscles before your workout, you might find that you become more productive in the time that you do dedicate to writing (in other words, five minutes of prep might make a single hour of writing more valuable than two hours with no prep at all).

Writer's Relief

When Copying Is Good For Your Career

It can be tough to keep yourself in a creative state of mind, especially when the world offers so many distractions. Every day, there's a new gadget to play with, a new TV show to watch, a new celebrity wedding. Plus, there are the distractions of personal life.

With so much going on, it can be hard to maintain a creative state of mind. Writers get stuck. If you're feeling distracted, and your ideas and enthusiasm for writing have dried up, consider taking a new approach: Copying for Creativity.

Of course, we don't mean plagiarizing (that's just gross and wrong!). We recommend choosing a passage word for word from a book or poem that you love and copying it into a favorite notebook. If possible, copy the passage by hand. Force yourself to copy slowly, to let the words sink in.

Set aside a few minutes a day for copying; even if you can't write, you can embrace the feel of writing, the rhythms of words, the creative energy that comes from reading an inspiring passage.

You know Newton's law stating that an object in motion stays in motion? Creativity can be like that. Ideas bring about more ideas. Writing brings about more writing.

So if you've stalled out, it may be time to get moving by copying a favorite passage into a notebook to get your creative juices flowing again.

Here's another element of copying to consider: Try rewriting your favorite works in your own words. Review a favorite scene in a book or story, then close the book and put it away. Rework it in your own voice, in your own way.

You may find that just getting started leads to new ideas. And who knows? If you follow your muse off on a tangent, you may find yourself with a wholly new work ready to be shined up and submitted for publication.

NOTE: We at Writer's Relief are NOT advocating plagiarism or literary theft. Any writing you submit to agents or literary journals must be entirely your own. If you copy a passage closely in any way, do so for private purposes only—in a journal or notebook.

And if you begin to rewrite a favorite scene to get your fingers tickling the keyboard, be sure that whatever you may submit from this practice exercise is wholly original and unique.

Memorization And Creativity

Finally, don't discount the power of memorization. Carry your favorite passage or poem around in your pocket, and look at it throughout the day.

When you really live with and inhabit a passage over a period of time, your experience of it deepens—and so does your own capacity for strong writing and creative thinking.

There's a reason teachers used to make students memorize poems back in the day. Memorizing a prose passage or poem not only builds memory skills, but it also increases creativity and interpretive powers as well.

Step Out Of Your Comfort Zone And Become A Better Writer

As creative writers, sometimes we need to stretch our muscles, step outside our stuffy little comfort zones, and try something new. Comfort zones are called just that because they are comfortable and safe. And while it's scary to do new things and take risks, it's the only way we grow.

We jump out of airplanes, talk to strangers at parties, and visit new countries when we want to face our fears and grow as people. But what can writers do to step out of their comfort zones and try something new? Here are a few ways to get started.

- Switch POV. Try writing a story in third person, even though you've always been most comfortable in first.

- Switch poetic forms. If you write narrative poetry, try a ballad, a palindrome, or a visual form of poetry. Or try your hand at romance if you normally write humor. Is there a writing style or form that has caused you problems in the past? Try it again and overcome your weakness.

- Take something ordinary and make it unusual. Write a story about something terribly boring but with a twist—your toaster oven comes to life, or something incredible happens when you open your mail.

- Try writing about something awkward, upsetting, embarrassing, or controversial. Tackle subjects like incest, religion, and STDs, or reveal your deepest, darkest secret in story form.

- Switch story settings and put yourself in unfamiliar situations. Attend an evangelical church if you're normally part of a super-sedate congregation—gain a new perspective on religion and how people worship. Or spend a few hours in an area of town you normally avoid and see it from a different view.

- Make a fool of yourself. Step onto a crowded elevator and stand facing the others rather than the door—really experience the feeling of awkwardness. What reactions do you get? Or plant yourself outside a large store and be an unofficial greeter—observe how people respond to you.

- Face a fear—and then write about it. Terrified of spiders? Visit the zoo and spend some hands-on time with some creepy crawlies. Or shut yourself in a closet and really tap into your claustrophobia.

Everyone feels more comfortable with what they know, and writers can easily fall into a habit of sticking to their comfort zones when it comes to literary form, genre, and theme. But these habits can block new and creative ideas. When a writer steps out of that comfort zone, either physically or in writing, there's no telling what will emerge!

Part Three

Rejection Letters

How To Make Rejection A Useful Tool

Examine Your Beliefs About Rejection

First things first: It's important to take a look at your own basic beliefs about rejection. You don't have to be a slave to negative feelings. The first step is knowing how to spot them. The second is knowing how to handle it when you do.

Writer's Relief

The Eight Rs Of Rejection

Reaction:
First, take a look at how you react to rejection. Do you wail and thrash about? Do you fall limply into bed, vowing never to write again? Do you snarl and immediately blame the stupid editor who failed to see talent when it fell right into his mediocre lap?

Or do you go back and look at your work to see if you followed submission guidelines to the letter? Was your cover letter error-free? Did you adhere to the maximum word count requirements? If all your "i's" were dotted and "t's" crossed, and you cannot find one thing wrong with your submission, then accept the gift of rejection from the editor-gods, and remember: Editors don't reject *you*—they are merely rejecting your work. And only *this* particular work for now. It is now time to go to the next step.

Release:
Do find a way to release your first reaction. There is no need to suppress hurt or anger, and doing so will only cause those feelings to fester. Feel free to foam at the mouth, yell at the wall, eat a pint of ice cream, or release your frustration in some way that is not harmful to you or your family.

Once you've vented your hurt feelings or anger, find a constructive way to release your rejection-reaction: exercise, talk it out with a friend, another writer, a writing group, throw darts at a picture of the editor or the front cover of the magazine from whence came the rejection.

Better yet, write a humorous article on—what else?— rejection! Laughter is always a great release, and your writer-friends will undoubtedly be able to relate to your experiences. Just be careful you're not falling into bitterness. Humor is great; bitterness can be toxic.

Resist:
Resist the temptation to wallow in the awful feeling of rejection. Resist the temptation to avoid your keyboard. Remind yourself that your manuscript was one of thousands upon thousands that didn't quite make the cut, and move on.

Once you've allowed yourself to go through the emotion of rejection and release in whatever ways work best for you, it's crucial to move past the grief. If you can't quite face the task of writing or revising your poems, stories, or the next great American novel, write inspirational or humorous letters to friends or family—just as long as you're writing something. It helps to restore your faith in yourself as a writer and reinforce confidence in your craft.

Look to others who can help you resist the urge to wallow. Find a mentor if you don't already have one. Join a writing group, or post your work online in a private group for fellow writers to critique. It's always good to have the support of someone who understands the writing life to lift you up when those rejections come. It's not a bad thing to commiserate with other writers before stepping back out into the cold and lonely world of the submission process. Whatever you do, don't wallow.

Release and then *resist* the temptation to let your career stall out.

"Talent is helpful in writing, but guts are absolutely essential."
—Jessamyn West

Recap:
Take a look at how far you've come. Going over your list of past successes can help soften the blows of a rejection. If you don't have a list of your past victories, make one. If you are not yet published, review your piece and see if you can rearrange it or expand it for a new market, taking into account what you've learned from others' criticisms or compliments. Go back to earlier manuscripts to review your own growth as a writer. If you don't see a difference in your writing, you might consider improving your skills by taking some writing workshops. And don't be afraid to rework a piece.

It's also a good idea to step back from your work a bit. Take a few days away from it. This can help give a fresh perspective for what needs changing. At the very least, your emotions need time to cool down so you can get a clearer perspective of what you already have and what may need changing.

Revisit the Market:
Take another look at the market in which you are trying to publish. Did you *really* send your piece to the right people? Remember: Successful submissions are about numbers (to a point). Don't give up after only a few tries. It takes lots of time and energy to get published.

Reach for Help:
Consider help from an editing service or a writing group. Writer's Relief has the expertise to help ensure your work is grammatically accurate and well-proofed. We know what editors and agents expect in regard to industry-standard formatting. We know who is and who is not reading. We spend countless hours tracking and reporting on this ever-changing information.

In addition, a good writing group provides more than support; members offer critique and ideas about how you can present your work in a different light. Carefully consider the comments from your fellow writers, and incorporate those suggestions that you find repeated most often. Study the market, read as much material by other writers in your genre as possible, and fortify yourself with knowledge—knowledge that will translate into confidence, which, in turn, will shine through in your work.

Repeat:
Continue to submit—not necessarily to the same editor right away, but certainly submit your work again, once you've deemed it clear, accurate, and usable. Even if you're a beginner, remember that it took time and patience to learn the multiplication tables as a child, but you eventually (hopefully) mastered them. Don't freeze like a deer in headlights with the shock of rejection. Go through whatever steps it takes to get your work back out there. There is no substitute for persistence.

Resilience:
Every successful writer must learn to develop the ability to recover and adjust easily to the rejection that is a necessary part of a successful submission strategy. Developing a thick skin to the submission process and rejections can be difficult. Well-known literary journals receive thousands of submissions and choose only a handful per issue.

What Does A Rejection Letter Mean?

Believe it or not, there is a secret language of rejection letters.

If you've been sending your work out for submission for a long time, then you know that rejections can start to look generic. However, there can sometimes be secret meanings in what your rejection letters are trying to tell you.

What rejection letters are *not* trying to tell you is that you should give up writing. So don't ever let yourself believe that's the case.

First, let's look at the different types of rejection letters:

The form-letter rejection

A form-letter rejection is easy to spot. This may be a short, generic note that reads something like, "Dear Writer—No thanks." Or "Dear Writer—Please try again."

There's not much to be learned from a blanket rejection letter. But a few literary journals do have "tiered" rejection letters: a) one form for writers they don't want to encourage; b) one for people who are good writers but who aren't a good fit; or c) one for writers who are invited to submit again.

Some literary agents or editors who do not use a form will simply send the work in question back with a handwritten note that says something like, "Not for us."

Standard phrases used in rejection letters from literary agents and editors of literary journals:

- Cannot use it/accept it at this time

- Didn't pique my interest
- Didn't strike a chord
- Doesn't meet our needs
- Doesn't fit our plans
- Have to pass on this
- Isn't resonating with me/us
- Isn't something we'd like to pursue
- No room for more clients (unless truly compelling)
- Not a right fit
- Not exactly what we're looking for
- Not for us
- Not suitable for us
- Not quite right for this list/publication
- We are not enthusiastic enough about this work
- We are not certain we could be effective in placing your work
- We are not right for your work
- We recommend you buy/subscribe/read our magazine
- We do not have a place/room for this
- and the list goes on!

If you receive a rejection letter with phrases like those above, be careful not to misinterpret it. A form letter doesn't mean you targeted your writing to the wrong agent or editor. It doesn't mean you've made a mistake by sending your submission. A form letter, no matter what the exact phrasing, is a nice, generic way of saying no thanks.

The personal rejection letter

When a literary agent or editor has taken the time to include a comment about your submission, then you know it's a personalized rejection.

Even if the comment is a critique of your work, we recommend you consider resubmitting to any literary agent or editor who cared enough about your work to offer a personal comment.

Send the agent or editor a thank-you note, and if/when you resubmit, reference the comments from the original rejection.

An invitation to resubmit

Some journals and literary agents always invite writers to submit again—it's part of their form rejection. But others make such an offer more cautiously. At Writer's Relief, we track our clients' rejections and acceptances, so we know when these kinds of comments are "boilerplate" phrases in a form letter and when they are personalized.

- We invite you to submit more in the future.
- Do you have anything else we can consider? Please send.

Why, you may wonder, are you being rejected if the writing is so great?

A piece may be rejected simply because the timing is off. Or your project was too similar to something else already in the works. Or the editor or agent might believe you have talent and he/she is looking forward to seeing you develop it.

Either way, send a thank-you note and a new submission (when possible), and again, reference the original comments in your cover/query letter.

Close, but not quite

Often, writers will begin to get discouraged when they get too many "near misses." But there's a valuable lesson to be learned if you're receiving rejections that imply "close but not quite."

Take the time to analyze any comments you've received. Is there a common thread (i.e., tired theme, flat characters, weak ending)?

When choosing to make revisions based on feedback, think carefully before you start taking every piece of advice thrown your way. Follow your heart and consider the comments thoughtfully—avoid knee-jerk reactions.

If one agent says "you should have written this in first person," you may want to wait to hear if any other agents have the same comment before making such a drastic revision. It's important to trust your instincts.

Keep in mind that what one agent dislikes, another agent might enjoy! That said, if you receive multiple comments that critique the same elements, it's certainly time to revise.

Finally, if you're getting many nice rejections, it may be time to reevaluate your submission strategy. Professional writers submit habitually and carefully—with proper etiquette and targeting. If you're not sure of exactly what's required by the industry, Writer's Relief can help you with that.

How Should Writers Deal With Rejection Letters?

Writing is a business, and writers must remember that agents and editors have nothing against them personally.

Agents'/editors' jobs depend on the choices they make, and if they don't feel the work will sell—or they simply don't feel any enthusiasm or passion for the piece—they don't have time to argue or explain exactly why.

Literary agents and editors of literary journals have different tastes and interests, which is why writers should learn what they can from rejection letters and then keep submitting to find the agent or editor who will love their work.

Here's a story about a client who is living proof that rejection isn't an end—it's sometimes just a means that inspires you to be the best you can be!

One day, one of our clients received a literary agent manuscript request. Honestly, this happens a lot in our office. What makes this particular request so inspiring is the backstory.

The writer's manuscript was originally submitted some time before. But there were no takers. While some writers might have been discouraged by dozens of rejections, this particular client held her head high.

Years passed. Determined to find a home for her book, she revised her manuscript, came up with a killer new title, and had us revise her query letter. Then, she resubmitted—to agents who hadn't seen the project and to a few who had.

And—surprise—there's been significant interest in the book!

Here's what got it done:

Determination: As writers, we will face seemingly endless rejections to our work. It is our task, however daunting, to remain strong-willed and determined.

Patience: Requests like this don't appear overnight. Time can be our greatest foe and our greatest ally.

Waiting: This is often the hardest part. Waiting for agents or journals to review our work is the best time to start on new work! Keep those creative juices flowing—and never ever stop.

Hope this will help inspire your day. It inspired ours!

Writer's Relief

Famous Author Quotes About Rejection From Agents And Editors

"I tell writers to keep reading, reading, reading. Read widely and deeply. And I tell them not to give up even after getting rejection letters. And only write what you love."
—Anita Diamant

"Every rejection is incremental payment on your dues that in some way will be translated back into your work."
—James Lee Burke

"I discovered that rejections are not altogether a bad thing. They teach a writer to rely on his own judgment and to say in his heart of hearts, 'To hell with you.'"
—Saul Bellow

"I think that you have to believe in your destiny; that you will succeed, you will meet a lot of rejection and it is not always a straight path, there will be detours—so enjoy the view."
—Michael York

"I could write an entertaining novel about rejection slips, but I fear it would be overly long."
—Louise Brown

"Was I bitter? Absolutely. Hurt? You bet your sweet ass I was hurt. Who doesn't feel a part of their heart break at rejection. You ask yourself every question you can think of, what, why, how come, and then your sadness turns to anger. That's my favorite part. It drives me, feeds me, and makes one hell of a story."
—Jennifer Salaiz

"You must keep sending work out; you must never let a manuscript do nothing but eat its head off in a drawer. You

send that work out again and again, while you're working on another one. If you have talent, you will receive some measure of success—but only if you persist."
—Isaac Asimov

"Beginning writers must appreciate the prerequisites if they hope to become writers. You pay your dues—which takes years."
—Alex Haley

"Literature is like any other trade; you will never sell anything unless you go to the right shop."
—George Bernard Shaw

"Mere literary talent is common; what is rare is endurance, the continuing desire to work hard at writing."
—Donald Hall

Writer's Relief

And Now, Here's How You Can Turn Acceptances Into Rejections
(Yes, You Read That Right!)

After years and years of watching our client list receive hundreds of acceptances per cycle, the staff of Writer's Relief finally understands what it's like to be, like…totally sick of all those positive responses from journals and agents. Who wants to get published anyway, right?

So if you loathe seeing your work in print and enjoy making paper castles out of all those form rejections, read on. We'll tell you the quickest ways to make sure you'll never have to look at an acceptance letter again!

1. We don't need no stinkin' cover letters. Surely your work can speak for itself. As long as you've scribbled your name and phone number somewhere on the page, you'll be fine. This works especially well for literary agents. They don't need a synopsis—and if they don't feel like looking you up in the phone book, that's their problem, not yours.

2. Formatting, schmormatting. One-inch margins and spell-check are for punks.

3. Send to every journal ever. Got a group of ten poems about inner-city Dumpster diving? If you're looking for that definitive, satisfying "NO," the best journals to send them to are those that have nothing to do with cities or Dumpsters. Send them to journals about nature and spirituality. Don't research literary journals. Accurate targeting is overrated anyway.

4. Hound the editors. Most people assume that editors are completely swamped with paperwork and emails day in and day out. Well, that's true…but who cares? After you've sent your awesomely raw (read: sloppy) work to editors, email them every day to confirm that they've received it. Send a couple of letters in the mail too, just to be sure. Or, even better, call! That'll really get 'em going.

The same thing goes for following up with literary agents; they hate being called. Go get their numbers on speed dial and go crazy!

5. Aim high. Like, really high. If you don't have any publication credits, the best way to continue that trend is to submit to the most prestigious, competitive literary journals out there. There's no sense in building up your bio and studying your craft. Sure, there are those rare occasions when someone unknown gets published in the *New Yorker*, but for the most part, your rejection is pretty much in the mail already. Yay!

6. Take it personally. In the event that all of these rejections start getting to you, take to your blog immediately and put every editor and/or literary agent who has rejected you on blast. Professionalism: Who needs it?

So, if you don't want to get acceptances, follow the steps above. Otherwise, try this:

Writer's Relief

Turn Rejections Into Acceptances

Do you have a stack of rejections sitting on your desk, taunting you? Develop a strategy that, when honed, will increase your chances of publication.

1. Practice, practice, practice.

It's nice to think that we are all naturally gifted writers from birth, but as with most creative pursuits, everyone has to practice. Your writing skill is like a knife. Sharpen it! The deeper you explore your talents and the more techniques you try, the better you'll be able to gauge where your strengths and weaknesses lie.

2. Write often and a lot.

A common mistake many new writers make is not having any backup. It's great to have a piece of work you're proud of, but you'll quickly run out of places to submit to if you send out the same stuff over and over again. If one particular piece isn't eliciting any positive responses, it might be time to switch it up and send something new.

3. Format and proofread thoroughly.

The importance of this step cannot be stressed enough. Make sure it's *perfect*! Editors and agents get hundreds of submissions passing across their desks every day, and one of the first lines of defense is to cut out the sloppy stuff. Spell-checker and grammar books are your friends! If proofreading isn't your forte, Writer's Relief proofreaders can help.

4. Do the research.

Research the best literary journals for your short prose and poetry, and research the best literary agencies for your books. You can't find the right places to submit your work without a little legwork. Do *not* send your work out to someone "just because." If you've been getting a lot of rejections, it may be because you're not submitting to the journals or agencies that are right for your work. Every editor and literary agent is different, and they're all looking for different things. Read the submission guidelines and take a look at the work they have published previously. If your work doesn't match up, don't waste your time. Move on!

FYI: We're not going to hard-sell you anything, but we do want to let you know one thing that can help. If you despise tedious hours of researching literary agents and magazines, Writer's Relief can research (and target) the best markets for your unique writing style and publishing goals. We've been helping writers successfully connect with agents and editors since 1994.

5. Have a killer cover or query letter.

Think of your cover letter as a handshake. When you meet someone, especially in a professional setting, you don't give him or her a limp, noodly handshake, do you? So why send out a weak and bland cover letter? Create one that is concise, professional, and efficiently informative. Show your confidence as a writer. Let your personality shine through. This is an editor's or agent's first impression of you, so make it a good one!

FYI: Writer's Relief can create your cover or query letter too! Put our expert submissions strategists to work for you!

6. Don't be afraid to start small.

Boy, wouldn't it be nice to get published in the *Paris Review* at the beginning of your career? Sure! We just wouldn't suggest holding your breath. We do recommend going for the smaller journals first, at least while you're starting out. Smaller publications are incubators for emerging writers and, best of all, they're *looking* for the new and unpublished! Be open to online journals as well, as they have gained a lot of popularity and respect over the years. Do that and you can...

7. Build your publication credits.

Once you start getting acceptances from smaller journals, more prestigious publications will look more favorably upon your work. It's not a matter of snobbery—a list of credits shows that not only is your work good, but there is a market for it. This also applies if you are seeking representation for a book. Publication credits in poetry or prose not only show your potential but also prove your versatility.

8. Track your submissions.

Keeping an updated list of your submissions and responses will give you a sense of the bigger picture. Editors or agents sometimes give constructive criticisms and feedback—keep note of these personal comments! When you're ready to submit again, these should be the first people you send to. You're on their radar. Take advantage!

9. Be honest with yourself.

Even the best writers can write mediocre stuff. It's a natural part of the creative process. And while it's not easy to admit that a piece of work isn't necessarily amazing, being honest with yourself about the quality of your work will help you in the end. Is your book query not getting the raves you expected? Step back and look at it objectively. Don't let your proximity to the work block your view of what might be improved.

And remember...

10. Don't take it personally.

Discouragement is a new writer's biggest enemy. It's easy to assume that if no one is accepting your work, you are an awful writer. Not true! Perseverance and patience are a must for writers: They are absolutely key when you're breaking into the writing industry. Literary agents and editors aren't sinister figures sitting behind flaming stacks of crappy writing—they're just doing their job, and they have nothing against you. So chin up!

Mental Strategies For Coping With Rejection

In the first part of this book, we talked about the mental and emotional strategies that will get you through the doldrums of the writing life.

Now, let's zoom in and focus on rejection. How can a writer learn to cope with the negative feelings that come when a rejection letter arrives in the mail?

Unfortunately, *this* is out of the question:

Dear Editor,

Thank you for your recent rejection of "The World's Best Story." While I receive dozens of rejections per day, it is not possible for me to respond to each one individually; hence, this form letter.

While your rejection was well-written and concise, the two words you sent ("no thanks") lacked substance and failed to address the specific reasons why my story was rejected. Therefore, I am unable to accept it, and I look forward to the publication of my story in a future issue of your magazine. I invite you to resubmit further rejections on new materials I send your way; however, please be aware that future rejections will be considered more readily if they are 1) polite, 2) constructive, and 3) personal.

Sincerely,
Writer

So you've got to have a plan B: a personal, internal way of dealing with rejection. This may sound familiar, but let's take a look at a few more mental techniques that will help you get by.

Learn To Detach

We mentioned before that it's helpful to take a look at how you react to being turned down, at your basic beliefs about rejection. This is a very personal issue. Yet at the crux of human vulnerability lies a universal truth. It's Zen in its simplicity. It's the truth of attachment.

Buddhists teach that attachment lies at the heart of all human suffering. Certainly this is true of a writer's work. After all, it's your creation, your child, birthed from the very depths of your being. It's part of who you are. And when your creation is rejected, it's as if your very *self* is rejected.

One of the most important things every writer must learn is to become unattached to the outcome—whether it's a rejection or an acceptance. This doesn't imply you don't care about publication or that you don't take it seriously. It means that if someone else rejects it, you don't have to believe they are rejecting you. And, in fact, they are not.

Writers who are engrossed in the process, in the art and craft of writing itself (and eventually, an entire submission strategy and implementation), understand that the end result is just that: an *extra bonus* born from a process they love. Their focus remains on the writing, the writing, the writing.

The more you can separate your inner being from the outer result of your writing, the more capable you will become of moving forward and onward after each rejection. In essence, the less attached you become to your work, the easier it will be to accept rejection and move forward. Ultimately, it will be easier to be persistent.

Retain A Sense Of Humor

So what to do with your rejections after you've finally, if not willingly, accepted them? Allow your creativity full rein here. It sure doesn't hurt to keep a sense of humor either.

It's no secret that being a writer means dealing with rejection letters. Whether a "no thanks" can be chalked up to an editor's personal taste or a submission that hit the right market at the wrong time, rejection is a rite of passage that we all experience.

Keep Moving Forward

We've given you some tips and strategies in this book for making stronger submissions; we hope you'll use them. Also, check out the many writers resources on our website, listed at the end of this book.

Knowing that you are always improving, always moving forward, always gaining new ground—*that* will keep you going. When you're consciously improving, you're building the momentum that will carry you toward your goals.

Some Final Thoughts

Ralph Keyes, author of *The Writer's Book of HOPE*, provides some good advice for all writers. He actually encourages writers to trust *themselves* over publishers in terms of the ultimate judgment of the work.

He notes that some editors have been "wrong" in publishing history and cites the rejections of John Grisham and Tom Clancy, among others who are now household names but who also faced lots of rejection.

Writers, like many other creative people, are sometimes too sensitive for their own good. We tend to see others' opinions of us as truth, particularly when the "other" carries the title of Editor, Publisher, or Agent. Of course, it makes sense to listen to the experts, and most of the time, writers benefit from doing just that. But just because some of them don't accept your work at any given time, doesn't mean they hold the truth of your writing career.

Again, look at all the angles. Once you are confident that your cover letter, query, proposal, and the work itself all check out accurately, you have to simply accept that it's the editor at that particular publication and time, not your work, that's the cause of the rejection.

And again, editors and agents aren't always right, nor are they always (almost never!) out to get you personally. A rejection of your work at a particular time is not a rejection of you, no matter how much it stings.

"You have to know how to accept rejection and reject acceptance."
—Ray Bradbury

Writer's Relief

Writer's Relief encourages you to think like an editor in order to help get you through the rejection part of the writing life. First, remember that editors are humans, like you, with varied likes and dislikes.

Think about how you select the books you like to read. You don't like every book or article you pick up, do you? One book may even determine whether or not you will read anything by the same author again. You may be interested in a subject a magazine runs one month, only to discover you think the author is too condescending or too wordy. Using this knowledge, accept the fact that even if your work fits a particular publication, it simply may not be the editor's taste.

It Bears Repeating: Don't Give Up. Be Persistent.

We cannot stress perseverance and resilience enough. If you allow your rejections to define you, you are apt to falter and perhaps even stop writing altogether. Don't let that happen.

You will have to search very hard to find well-known authors who never felt the blows of rejection. We all know the fantastic story of first-time acceptance of first-time submission that rumors its way round writers' circles. This is the exception, *not* the rule.

For most writers, *this* is the rule: Keep writing, and keep submitting! Start your next piece even while you are waiting to hear back from other submissions. If your novel is circulating, start another; finish a story and start another. Keep writing, and keep submitting!

If writing is about what you will earn, you may want to reconsider your career. But if writing for you is about who you are, what you love—if you believe it would be like someone severing your limb if you were not allowed to write—welcome to the writing world and all that comes with it.

Believe in yourself; don't count on editors and agents to do it for you. Yes, there will be some, maybe even many, who will believe in you and your work and help keep you going. Only *you* get to reside inside your head and heart every day. You are the one to decide just how you will react to the responses you receive; you are the one who will decide what you will do with both rejection and success. Make both count!

"As a younger man I wrote for eight years without ever earning a nickel, which is a long apprenticeship, but in that time I learned a lot about my trade."
—James Michener

We encourage you to look at rejection from this point of view: If you aren't getting rejected, you aren't getting your work out there to be read.

In the world of writing, three things are certain:
- If you submit your work, you will receive rejections.
- If you do NOT, your work will NOT be accepted if it is not read.
- Every rejection brings you one step closer to acceptance.

The choice is yours.

"I have learned that success is to be measured not so much by the position that one has reached in life as by the obstacles which he has overcome while trying to succeed."
—Booker T. Washington

Part Four

Guide To Writer's Relief Author Resources

Resources On Our Website

Submit Write Now! Our weekly e-publication features interviews, news, strategies, tips, publishing leads, contests, and so, so much more!

Writers Classifieds Pages Find lists of publishing leads, contests, calls for submissions, anthologies, writing conferences, etc.

Publishing Tool Kit Our tool kit answers just about every question you might have about how to develop a successful submission strategy. Get your tool kit today! Here are some of our topics:

- How To Get Published: A Step-By-Step Guide For Beginning And Intermediate Writers
- Grammar And Usage
- Short Story Submissions: How To Submit Short Stories For Publication
- Poetry Submissions: How To Submit Your Poetry For Publication
- Query Letters: Everything You Must Know To Dazzle Literary Agents
- Literary Agent Submissions: How To Find Representation For Your Book Project
- Web Design: Online Marketing And Promotion Strategies For Writers
- Self-Publishing: Everything You Need To Know About Self-Publishing
- How To Handle Rejection: A Writer's Secret Weapon Against Rejection
- Writers Associations: Local And National Organizations For Writers

Video Tutorials for people who aren't sure how to make submissions using e-mail or online submission managers.

Free consultation with a submission strategist. See if Writer's Relief has a plan that will work for your submissions to agents or lit mags.

PLUS—Are You Ready To Develop Your Author Platform?

Sign up on www.WebDesignRelief.com to get your free report, "The Writer's Essential Guide To Reputation-Building In A Digital World," today! We are experts in designing websites specifically for authors. Check it out!

Having a website is an essential strategy; it's no longer optional for serious writers who want to make a name for themselves.

We know what works for author websites. And we're the *best* value on the Web for writers. We know—we did the research.

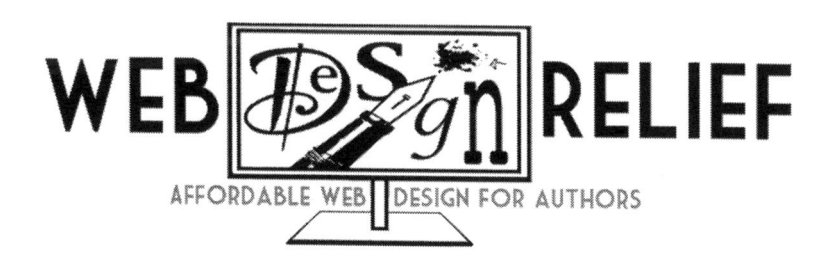

Our Invitation To You

Congratulations! You've finished reading *The Happy Writer* and have learned a lot about how to overcome the emotional pitfalls of the writing life.

You now have the tools to find balance in your personal journey and to remain healthy and productive as you deal with the challenging aspects of a writer's life. We hope you'll refer to *The Happy Writer* whenever you need to get back on track.

Please reach out to us with your questions or if you need help building a healthy submission strategy.

Keep writing and submitting!

Ronnie L. Smith, President
Ronnie L. Smith and the Staff of Writer's Relief
www.WritersRelief.com
(866) 405-3003

Made in the USA
Lexington, KY
01 February 2014